INSIDE YOUR THERAPIST'S MIND

How A Psychotherapist Thinks, and Why It Works

DR. DREW E. PERMUT

Copyright © 2012 Dr. Drew E. Permut

All rights reserved.

ISBN: 1479302694

ISBN 13: 9781479302697

Library of Congress Control Number: 2012917189
CreateSpace Independent Publishing Platform
North Charleston, South Carolina

For Deborah

My wife, my colleague, my most trusted advisor, my most passionate supporter

TABLE OF CONTENTS

Acknowledgments vii

Introduction ix

Chapter 1. Understanding the Psychotherapy Process 1

Chapter 2. Medicine, Psychology, and the Problem of Diagnosis 21

Chapter 3. The Making of a Psychotherapist 33

Chapter 4. The Psychotherapy Relationship 47

Chapter 5. Addiction and Recovery 55

Chapter 6. Therapist Errors and What They Mean 71

Chapter 7. Why Psychotherapy Takes Time 81

Chapter 8. How Therapy Heals 95

ACKNOWLEDGMENTS

Writing a book involves many hours of solitary contemplation, but it cannot be accomplished without the support and inspiration of others. I had often thought about writing a book about psychotherapy, but I needed my family's encouragement to actually express my thoughts on the printed page. This process evolved slowly over time. When my children were young they had other aspirations for me. My daughters wanted to me to compete on Jeopardy, my sons thought I should apply for the position of Commissioner of Baseball. Only when they were older did they give voice to the idea that I should write a book. My wife, who is also a psychotherapist and who understands my work better than anyone, strongly seconded the idea. Without all this encouragement, I am certain this book would not have been written.

My colleagues have been a second source of inspiration. Psychotherapists spend much of their time alone with their patients, in an intensely interesting, but private world. Having a community of colleagues with whom I can share ideas, raise questions, and develop a deeper understanding of myself and of my work has become an essential part of my life. I am fortunate, of course, to be married to a colleague. But I also have good friends in the profession, particularly those whom I have met at the Washington School of Psychiatry. Their enthusiastic encouragement of this project and willingness to read many drafts of book chapters has made it possible for me to find just the right voice for communicating my ideas and experiences.

Perhaps most of all, I have drawn inspiration from my patients. The process of confronting fears and changing life-long patterns of behavior is difficult, time-consuming, and often painful. And yet, I have seen hundreds of people whose courage and integrity enabled them to make these difficult changes. These are stories that need to be told, to help others see how pain and dysfunction can be worked through and lives transformed by psychotherapy. After careful deliberation, I gave several of my patients chapters to read, asking them if they thought I had adequately captured the essence of the therapy process. Their positive reactions and thoughtful feedback have helped me fine-tune my writing and address some of the issues they thought most needed to be explained.

Finally, a special thank you to Annabelle and Mal Powell, Tim Smith, Zach Conrad, Jordan Conrad, Brian Robinson, Melanie Maholick and Ken Fox whose careful reading, comments, and editing helped to make this book a reality.

INTRODUCTION

As a psychotherapist, I often have to prepare myself before certain social situations, like cocktail parties. It's not that I don't like to socialize; I'm actually a fairly gregarious person. But I know that it's very likely I'll be asked one of these questions:

"You're a psychologist – does that mean you're analyzing me the whole time we're talking?"

"How do you turn your analyzing off when you come home from work?"

"I've heard that nobody takes Freud seriously anymore. Isn't that right?"

These questions always put me in a quandary. On the one hand, they reveal a fundamental misconception of what I do, and what it means to be a psychotherapist. On the other, if I really want to respond candidly, I would need much more time than I'm sure anyone wants to spend listening to me drone on about my profession. It would even bore me.

Still, the frequency with which these questions are asked makes it clear that there is a need to demystify and understand what psychotherapy is – and isn't – about. In writing this book, I hope to help you understand what it means to be in therapy, both from the patient's perspective and the therapist's. Among the issues I will address are:

- Taking you inside the thought processes that a psychotherapist engages in
- Showing you how it's not the psychotherapist, but you that controls the therapy

- How diagnoses are made
- How a particular kind of approach is chosen,
- Why psychotherapy often takes so long and costs so much
- Why the therapist is not really a neutral observer and how that can help you
- Why just talking to a good friend often doesn't help you with your problems
- Why medications are not a substitute for psychotherapy

There are a few things about me you need to know in order to better understand what psychotherapy is and how it works. My professional training is in Clinical Psychology, which involves the science and application of psychological principles to the diagnosis and treatment of patients. As part of my doctoral training, I spent many years learning to administer and interpret psychological tests, provide psychotherapy to individuals, couples, families, and groups, and both perform and interpret relevant research. This was a five-year process, all under constant supervision of other psychologists. Not all psychotherapists come from this professional background. Psychiatrists first go to medical school, then do a one year medical internship and then a three-year residency in psychiatry, which usually focuses on the biological and pharmacological aspects of mental disorders. Clinical Social Workers also perform psychotherapy, but their training is often shorter (two years in most cases), less research-focused, and does not involve training in testing. This does not mean that in all cases I am better trained than psychotherapists from other related disciplines. But I have found the unique combination of intensive theoretical, scientific, and clinical training fundamental to the approach I bring to my work with patients.

Professional training, however, is only one component of a skilled psychotherapist. Equally important is the therapist's own experience as a psychotherapy patient. Not everyone in the field would agree with this, but my deep conviction is that psychotherapists cannot adequately master the intricacies of psychotherapy without their own very thorough analysis. This is a humbling, but necessary admission; every therapist shares problems in common with his or her own patients. It isn't that we are fundamentally different from or better than our patients. It is that in addressing our own psychological problems, we

INTRODUCTION

learn essential things about ourselves, our emotions, our blind spots, our defenses. If we take the time not only to examine these issues but work them through, we have an entire layer of knowledge to transmit to our patients that we could not know about any other way. And we also know what it means and feels like to be a patient, which allows us to be more sensitive and attuned to the people who come to us for help.

My own experience as a psychotherapy patient is both long and broad – over twenty years in total, involving individual, group, and couples therapy. In all honesty, I needed every bit of it. Like most psychotherapists that I have known, my family of origin was quite dysfunctional. When I first entered psychotherapy in my twenties, I knew that I was suffering from considerable anxiety. It was only as the process unfolded over many years that I was able to see how many ways my thoughts and feelings were distorted by my earlier experiences. Going through a long, deep analysis of myself enabled me not only to feel better (most of the time) which had been my initial concern, but to understand and actually change the way I thought and felt in a much healthier direction. When my patients approach the end of a successful therapy process by sharing with me how transformed they feel, I know just what they mean.

One other aspect of my background must be mentioned. As you read this book, you will no doubt notice that I am not neutral about my beliefs and conceptualizations. I have a very defined viewpoint, which is derived from what is known as psychodynamic theory, a refinement and advancement of earlier Freudian concepts. In the most basic terms, this means that my work is generally informed by attention to the importance of childhood and adolescent experiences, unconscious motivations, and repetitions of earlier conflicts in present-day relationships. However, I am not a very orthodox practitioner of the psychodynamic approach to psychotherapy. Theories are necessarily simplifications of data, and do not explain everything. Sometimes, in fact, they turn out to be wrong. An open-minded psychotherapist, much like the scientist many of us were trained to be, is obliged to pay attention to all the data, even that which disconfirms prior beliefs. Other points of view often turn out to better explain this data, and can helpfully instruct the therapist in the development of a broader theoretical viewpoint, which in turn increases the tools available to assist the patient. This is why more experienced clinicians are often more versatile and skillful therapists; if they are honest and self-aware, they have much more knowledge of both theory and technique.

This book is, of course, no substitute for the psychotherapy experience itself. A book about psychotherapy can only approximate the actual process. Moreover, everybody's situation is in some essential way unique. A useful analogy may be of the relation between a very good movie and actual life: it is suggestive, but in no way intended to give a perfect, complete representation of the real thing. Still, in addressing many of the basic issues that come up in psychotherapy, you may become more aware of the possible uses and benefits that it can provide. If you, or someone close to you is contemplating entering psychotherapy, you will certainly be a more informed consumer. And if I should meet you at a cocktail party, we'll have a lot to talk about.

1. UNDERSTANDING THE PROCESS

How Psychotherapy Works

To understand what actually happens in the deep form of therapy known as psychodynamic psychotherapy, it may be most helpful to provide a few clinical examples. These are derived from people I've actually seen in my practice, though I've changed enough details to ensure that their privacy is protected. As I discuss these cases, I'll try to give you a sense for both what the patients were saying and feeling and what I, in turn, was thinking and feeling as I was interacting with them.

JIMMY

Jimmy was 31 years old when he first came to see me. He had been referred by a colleague who had seen him once for a brief employee assistance evaluation, and had the sense that I would work well with him. Though Jimmy had never seen a psychologist before, he apparently trusted the referring clinician's judgment enough to call me.

For the first appointment, Jimmy arrived early, and when I opened the door from my office to the waiting room, stood up and greeted me in a soft-spoken, friendly manner. His face had a slight smile and he made direct eye contact with me right away. I invited him into the office, where he quickly looked around and made a joke about all the different choices of seating. When I suggested he sit wherever he felt comfortable, he chose the easy chair farthest away from me.

Looking at him from across the room, Jimmy made a striking impression. He was a tall, athletic-looking man, meticulously dressed in a dark tailored suit, starched white shirt, and silk necktie despite the fact that this was the middle of a hot, sticky Washington summer. He looked every bit the successful law partner, which in fact, he had just become. Curiously, his depression seemed to have begun almost immediately upon becoming a partner in his firm. As he explained, he had been very driven to succeed, piling up enormous numbers of billable hours for years, all in the determination to become a success as soon as possible. Once he achieved this goal, he began to feel unexplainably sad and uninterested in anything, as though he was just going through the motions of his life. His friends would call, and he usually declined their invitations. Much of the time, he would daydream about living somewhere else, working in a bookstore, and living a simple life. All of this was relayed to me in a soft-spoken, unemotional tone. The only indication of deeper feeling came when he stood up at one point to remove his suit jacket, and I saw large sweat rings underneath his arms, and perspiration all over his face.

I asked him, as I often do in the first hour, if he could tell me something about his background. He told me he had grown up out West, in a very poor farming community. His father died in a car accident when Jimmy was a young child, and he had virtually no memories of him. To support him and his two younger siblings, his mother worked long hours, and was rarely at home. His maternal grandmother was the person who provided most of the childcare, and was the true parental presence in the family. He described her as absolutely devoted to the children, but exceedingly strict. Physical punishment was not uncommon. She set high standards for proper behavior, church attendance, and especially school achievement. Though he had some rebellious moments in adolescence, mostly he followed her rules, and was always a top student, graduating as class valedictorian. He subsequently went on to receive a full scholarship to an Ivy League university, where he

1. UNDERSTANDING THE PROCESS

was similarly successful. He was the first child from his family to even attend college, and one of only a very few from his entire neighborhood.

As the hour was drawing to an end, I was trying to make sense of all he had said, as well as what my experience had been with him during this first session. I was touched by his earnestness, sincerity, good manners. And yet, it was undeniably sad to be with him. I was trying to picture what his daily life might look like, and it all seemed dreary and empty. It was even a bit hard to listen to him; I found myself drifting from time to time as he spoke.

At this point, you might find yourself wondering how a psychotherapist could seem so judgmental or non-sympathetic to a patient in obvious distress. I should clarify what I mean by my comments about how I felt listening to Jimmy. That I found myself drifting was in no way a criticism of him. I had enormous respect for him as a person, and found him intensely interesting. Nor was it a matter of me having a bad day, of being too tired or preoccupied to attend carefully. Rather, whenever a therapist has a strong reaction of any kind to a patient it is a signal that a kind of unconscious communication is taking place. In other words, how it felt to be with Jimmy had some particular meaning, a kind of clue to what might be happening with him below the surface of conscious awareness.

An essential part of the training of a dynamically-oriented psychotherapist is to question how the patient is affecting you. In order to understand this, therapists must develop the capacity to observe their own emotional responses and thought processes in reaction to what the patient is saying. People communicate consciously with words; they communicate unconsciously with gestures and how they make you feel or think. The competent therapist must listen both to the patient and to him or herself in order to obtain a complete reading of what the patient is communicating. Sometimes the words do convey the message. But almost as often, patients communicate the deeper meaning of their experience through a mechanism known as *projective identification*.

Projective identification is an unconscious defense mechanism by which people essentially inject their feelings into you, as though they come from within you rather than from themselves. You usually don't know it's happening and neither do they. But if negative judgments about themselves seem to come from you, not them, they can hide from themselves what they really feel. The defense works like this:

> I don't want to admit I might feel angry/frightened/aroused/jealous/disgusted/lonely/despairing... It's too disturbing to know that about myself. I'll transfer those feelings into you so you can feel them. That way, I can deny that these are my feelings, and if you somehow express these thoughts or feelings, you're the one who's angry/frightened/aroused, certainly not me.

An example of this from everyday life is not hard to find. For example, think about a time when you were at an airport or in a busy store, and the ticket agent or clerk was indifferent or rude to you, not so much by what they said as in their unpleasant facial expression or manner. You might feel angry, but if you express it, it looks as though you are the one who has a problem with anger. The clerk is probably entirely unaware of having made you feel this way. What you are feeling is *their* anger, projected into you.

When I noticed how strong and consistent the feelings I was having with Jimmy were, I knew that this might be important information about what he might be feeling without his knowing it. I therefore took this feeling of mine as an unconscious communication from him. *It was not my dreariness or emptiness that I was feeling - it was his.* That's what he was unable to say, but I could decode through my tuning in to how he was affecting me.

I said to him: "I think your depression makes sense. You were raised by your grandmother to be very focused on working hard, and making something of yourself. Now that you've achieved that goal, you may be at a loss to know what else you want for yourself, or even who else you are. It's kind of an empty feeling not to know." His response was indirect, but very emotional. He smiled slightly, then said "She was tough," and his eyes began to well up. I decided not to comment on what I had just seen, so as not to make him self-conscious. Instead, I

1. UNDERSTANDING THE PROCESS

merely suggested that in working together we might be able to help him understand himself better, and decide what he really wants in life.

Jimmy and I spent many years together working in psychotherapy. Much of the time, it felt very slow and undramatic. More than with most people, I allowed long periods of silence to continue within the sessions. I sometimes wondered, momentarily, if I wasn't doing enough or saying enough to help him. But I actually knew that it was important for me not to be too active; my silences and seeming inactivity were quite deliberate. I knew from his history and my experience with him that he was struggling with two contradictory feelings: to be understood and cared for without having to ask for it, and to be free to make choices without interference or the worry of disapproval. In other words, he needed my help more than he could admit, but at the same time needed to feel that his choices were entirely his own. The only way to accomplish these two goals was to be quietly supportive, as he found his own self-definition.

Jimmy pursued the process faithfully, and over time, his life markedly improved. He began, for the first time in his life, to pursue romantic relationships, and after a few expected mis-steps, had two very significant, intimate relationships that he found satisfying. In the course of treatment, his grandmother became ill and eventually died; we were able to work through his complicated grief during this time, and give him a better sense of resolution about the role she played in his life, both good and bad. He also left his firm, and was able to develop a more balanced work and personal life, that didn't focus so exclusively on achievement.

By the time he completed his therapy with me, Jimmy was undeniably happier and functioning better in the world. Still, it was a bit odd for me at our departure. I felt happy for him that he was doing so well. But I did not feel satisfied that I had done my best work with him. I found myself wishing that I had given him more deeply insightful interpretations of his life experiences, so that I could be sure of what I had given him. This feeling, however, was actually a sign of how well the therapy had gone. He was able to leave happily because he felt the changes had to do with him, not me. It's a feeling familiar to parents of a child leaving home; it has to be the child's accomplishment, not yours.

Many years later, on the night before his wedding day, he sent me a note that read:

"I'm thinking of you on this special occasion. Everything has worked out so well for me. I honestly don't know where I would be without you."

So, how are we to understand or explain what happened in this psychotherapy experience? Clearly, it was not an example of dramatic technique or insight. In fact, I would say it was about only one early, basic insight. This was a man who was raised to believe in the importance of external self-definition: perfect behavior, perfect achievement, and perfect appearance. But it did not feel like a choice; it was demanded of him. I could tell from his demeanor and the way I felt in his presence that this was all empty for him, that what was missing was a sense of himself as a person. I could not provide this missing part for him by teaching, explaining, or directing him. Rather, I would have to be a quiet, but supportive presence who could encourage him to value his own internal feelings and judgments. His grandmother had given him so much: loved him fiercely, allowed him to rise out of poverty, and to learn the value of self-discipline. But she had also, unintentionally, crushed his sense of self out of her fear that he would fail. I would need to de-emphasize the external markers of identity that mattered so much to her, and help him discover the more personally meaningful, private thoughts that allowed him to feel good about himself on his own terms. That is why I deliberately took such a passive role throughout our work together. It had to be all about him, and I had to willingly and consciously detach myself from anything that I myself might want or need him to do.

CAROL

Carol was a 42 year old divorced college professor who was referred by a local university health center. She had come to the clinic initially because of severe headaches and digestive distress; once she had been checked out medically, they suggested she contact me because of her high level of stress and difficulty sleeping.

Carol was several minutes late for the first appointment. When she came into the waiting room, I came out of my office to greet her, as I usually do. She was in tears, apologizing repeatedly for her lateness, and commenting that she was "a total mess." I tried to reassure her that coming late to a psychologist was not uncommon, because it is such a difficult decision for many people. But she continued to berate herself, saying she should have given herself more time to get there, that she shouldn't be wasting my valuable time by being so inconsiderate.

I asked her to come in and tell me what going on that brought her to see me. She told me she had recently broken up with her boyfriend. They'd been seeing each other for about six months, and were beginning to talk about living together, but as they got closer to making that decision, she felt he was becoming more distant. She began to feel uncomfortable with their sexual relationship; she couldn't relax with him, and everything felt harsh and abrupt. Just about the time she was thinking of postponing the decision to move in together, she found his email correspondence with another woman, which was very flirtatious. When she confronted him with it, he became enraged about her "spying" on him (though he'd actually left his mailbox open), and began a blistering attack on her, accusing her of being controlling, uptight, and boring. She felt very badly about prying, and tried to explain what had happened, but he just stormed off. The next day, he emailed her that he wanted to come over to get his things from her apartment. Though she begged him to talk things over, he refused. They'd only had a few short email exchanges since. She tried to reach out to his friends to try to break through to him, but they mostly told her he had "moved on", and maybe she should too.

As she spoke, I noticed that Carol seemed extremely tense. Her right hand was clutching a throw pillow, her posture was stiff, her voice sounded tight and agitated. She talked almost non-stop, but mostly it was about what she had done wrong. I would have expected someone in her circumstances to be furious, but the only anger she expressed was about how stupid she was, how she should have paid more attention to him, how maybe she is boring, that her ex-husband also got tired of her. When I tried to suggest that perhaps the problems were not just hers but might equally be about his fears and conflicts, she seemed not to hear me at all, but kept criticizing herself for ruining things. I actually tried to interject my view several times, but I never got any sense that she understood my comments.

By the end of the first interview, I usually try to summarize what I believe are the fundamental issues underlying the patient's problems. But Carol's difficulty hearing even slightly supportive comments made me cautious about pushing too hard. So I simply suggested that it sounded like she was really struggling and that I thought by talking things out with me we could help her feel better.

For the first several weeks, I mostly just listened to her pain. As it turned out, her relationships were not the only area of her life that were causing her distress. At work, she had an unusually high teaching load, many committee assignments, and demanding deadlines for journal publications. Sleep was a torment; she would collapse in exhaustion most nights, but by 4:00 or so most mornings she awoke feeling worried that she was behind in her work, or not doing enough. One of the problems was that she never knew when she might have a "killer headache" that would put her out of commission for a day or two at a time. She would get behind in her work, and then have to work even harder to keep up. I asked her, gingerly, whether there might be something she could do to reduce her workload, since it sounded like it was becoming a real source of stress for her. This produced a torrent of insistence that it was impossible to make those kinds of requests, that the field was so competitive, that I had no understanding about what her situation was really like, that I was lucky to have the luxury of my own practice. I didn't ask again for a while, but I was struck by how much emotion she had in what she was saying. And that for the first time, I could see something approaching anger or resentment that was not aimed at herself.

I also began to feel what was behind Carol's over-conscientiousness, her excessive apologizing, her lack of confidence. As patients often do, she was unconsciously projecting these feelings into me, to keep them out of her awareness. As a result, I was feeling her unconscious

1. UNDERSTANDING THE PROCESS

experience when I was with her: a degree of tenseness, feeling tentative, somewhat powerless, and vaguely irritated at not being able to do my job. I caught myself thinking that it was a good thing that I didn't have too many other patients like her. I was aware that this was also an unconscious communication of her experience: "people don't really like me or don't want to be around me."

Largely because she was so guarded and defensive, I waited much longer than I typically would to ask about her family background. When I did inquire, her account was, unsurprisingly, guarded and defensive- and also reflected the defense mechanism of *denial*. With denial, disturbing facts or thoughts are either glossed over or misinterpreted in an unrealistically positive direction. The point of the defense is to allow the person to believe what they need to believe rather than what is actually true but disturbing. Here is how she described her childhood:

I grew up in a large Midwestern city, the only child of hard-working parents who wanted the best for me. You know, they had grown up in the Depression, so they were pretty serious, but I never wanted for anything. My father was a physician, and he was very respected in the community. I couldn't go anywhere without people saying what a wonderful doctor he was. My mother had been a nurse, and they met in a hospital when he was first starting out. But when they had me, they both decided it would be best for Mom to stay home to take care of me. A lot of nights, my father had to work late, but we all knew that he was a doctor who had people counting on him. So we would eat earlier, but always have dinner waiting for him, and we'd join him at the dinner table when he got home. Then we would listen to his stories about what had happened in his day, and maybe he would help me with my homework while Mom cleaned up and got ready for the next day. I suppose a lot of people would say it was kind of boring, but it was kind of like a 50s family, you know.

From the sound of it, a pretty unremarkable history. But, given her symptoms - harsh self-criticism, chronic anxiety, tension headaches, difficulty standing up for herself - not quite believable. Our personalities don't just develop out of genetic selection or bad luck. Almost always, who we become reflects something essential about our family experience. So while I didn't challenge what she had said, I knew there had to be a lot of missing pieces that she was unable to tell me- or even herself.

Over time, quite a long time actually, what emerged was a quite different story. Her father was a well-respected doctor in the community, but when he came home at night he was usually tired, irritable, and demanding. He did sit at the dinner table with them, but he talked only about himself, barely expressing interest in either Carol or her mother. When he did interact with his wife, it was usually to criticize something she had done or failed to do around the house. He did go over Carol's homework with her, but that really was about the only thing about her that he seemed interested in. And, of course, his comments about her work were often very harsh. Her mother did clean up while Carol did her homework with her father, but as she got older, Carol began to find hidden bottles in the kitchen, and several times found her mother so drunk she had to help her into her bed.

It was not easy to get this information from Carol. I had to ask very carefully, questioning whether, perhaps, such-and-such incident might have been different from what she remembered. Even when she could acknowledge a negative or disturbing aspect of her parents' behavior, it was almost always followed by a protective explanation such as "they did the best they could." Or, at times she would question my focus on the past, reminding me that after all, she's an adult now, and isn't it time we stop blaming her parents for everything. This made her progress very slow.

But I knew her very well by now, and understood that she wasn't trying to be difficult; it was the only way she knew to protect herself from feeling bad about her family and herself. That is a very important distinction. When therapists understand a patient's personality dynamics and motivations, it allows them to put the patient's behavior within the sessions into a sympathetic context. Carol's seeming irritation or impatience with me, or her rejection of a suggestion or interpretation I might make was not a rejection of me, or even the process. She was afraid. Knowing this, I could be patient, I could empathize with how difficult it must be to reexamine her past, I could accept her as she was. One of the ways that I knew she understood this acceptance, at least unconsciously, was that she was no longer focused on being good or trying to please me; she now felt the freedom to express anger at me, if she felt it, without fear of retaliation.

During this time, I could see that there were telltale signs of valuing what therapy was providing her, and steady improvements in her emotional and physical well-being. She never missed her appointments, and in spite of her complaints did seem to be feeling better. Her sleep was improving, and her headaches were occurring much less frequently, and were far less severe. I didn't really need her to tell me explicitly that she was feeling better. That might have put the focus on my needs or my approval of her. It was enough that I could see it

Several years into her therapy, I made an unintentional mistake with her. She had to go out of town during our regular appointment time, so she asked me if we could reschedule our session that week. I found a time that worked for both of us, and we agreed to meet then. When the appointment time arrived, it happened that I had forgotten I'd already scheduled the hour for another patient, weeks earlier. I'd simply forgotten to write it down in my main appointment book. I stepped out into the waiting room, and both my patients were sitting there, expecting to see me. The other patient took out the appointment card I'd written for him for this time. I said to them: "Obviously, I screwed this up. Is there any way one of you can come back at another time?" The other patient said this was the only time all week he could make it. Carol politely offered to come at a different time the next day. I thanked her for her flexibility, and told her that of course, I would not charge her for that session. She said she couldn't accept that; I insisted it was the least I could do for inconveniencing her.

When I did see her the next day, something had changed. It was subtle, but you could tell she was less resistant to my questions, somehow less fearful. Over the next few months, it began to feel like a more collaborative process. I could think more freely and share my reactions and questions with her without having to brace for her defensive responses. For the first time, we could occasionally laugh at something together. And slowly, she began to remember more about what actually happened at home, and how she felt, without having to immediately defend or cover-up her parents' behavior.

From the nature of this change in her interactions with me, it was clear that she experienced my error in an unmistakably positive way. She saw that I was embarrassed, but also that I admitted it was my fault. I think that her earlier guardedness came from seeing me in much the same way as her parents: an authority who would either hurt her or not protect her. She must have expected me to blame her in some way for the mix-up. When I did the opposite, she was both relieved and deeply moved.

This incident was a tipping point, but not the true source of the change in her. What had been going on, slowly, incrementally, almost imperceptibly was the development of trust and rapport that became the foundation for her eventual breakthrough. (It's a bit like the old joke about the Hollywood actor who becomes an "overnight success" after twenty years in the business). It was essential that I patiently sat with her, week after week, not pushing her too hard, but accepting the discomfort and even a little frustration of how slowly she needed to go. My acceptance of this situation was a way of accepting her. More than anything else, and certainly more than she could ever say, that is what she most needed - to feel acceptable, to not have to try so hard or be so good.

Carol's progress in her life began to mirror the changes in the therapy process. She began setting more limits on her work hours, refusing to take on extra assignments that someone else in the department could easily do as well. She began making friendships and personal relationships more of a priority in her life, something she found easier to do because she felt more relaxed with others. I could also see how different she looked physically: less tension in her body, posture that was less stiff, even a lighter, easier way of talking.

We continued to work together in therapy for several more years, in what became a very deep, thorough reworking of her sense of self. By the time we ended, she was nothing like the anxious, tormented young woman who first showed up in my waiting room.

These two case studies help to show some of the complexity of the psychotherapy process. Every patient is different, so that a competent therapist always has to adapt his or her way of working to fit the needs, temperament, and issues that the individual patient brings to the

1. UNDERSTANDING THE PROCESS

situation. For example, Carol and Jimmy were obviously quite different people. What I had to offer each of them was not a specific treatment protocol dispensed uniformly, like a medication in a prescribed dosage. Rather, it was completely non-standard: a highly individualized way of listening, understanding, and interacting that helped them feel heard and made it possible for them to change in their own time and way.

Although every psychotherapy experience is in some ways unique, it does not follow that it is a free-form process. On the contrary, there are a number of general rules that guide successful therapy. These may be thought of as the underlying structure of the psychotherapy process.

1. Psychotherapy involves both careful deliberation and spontaneity.

From the very first contact, every step of the treatment is carefully thought out, but not in a predetermined way. The treatment requires that the therapist maintain a careful discipline of allowing the observation of the patient's actual behaviors, thoughts, and emotions to dictate the interventions he or she will choose to employ. In this sense, it is quite similar to the discipline of a scientific investigation. But this commitment to unbiased observation does not mean that the therapy process becomes cold and clinical. In actual practice, each therapy session spontaneously unfolds from the interactions between the therapist and patient, informing the therapist at any given moment what to ask, how to ask it, when to speak, when to remain silent, how to understand what the patient is expressing either verbally or through various non-verbal communications. It should always feel human and relational, because the therapist is actively engaged as a person.

This combination of disciplined observation and spontaneous interaction is related to the particular kind of objectivity that therapists maintain. When we say that a therapist is objective, it does not imply that they are emotionally detached from the patient. In fact, quite the opposite is true. Only by being emotionally engaged, can the therapist accurately observe and understand the patient's deeper communications. The therapist needs to feel as well as hear and see the patient. Objectivity comes from years of careful training, in which the therapist learns to be aware of how he or she feels with the patient from moment to moment, and then analyze what that feeling may signify about the patient's personality, emotional conflicts, or strengths.

2. **Therapists must know their patients' histories to truly understand their present problems.**

As the American philosopher, George Santayana once famously said, "those who do not understand the past are condemned to repeat it." He was speaking of countries and societies, but his observation is equally true about individuals. Most of us would probably prefer to think that we have a great deal of choice in how we act, think and feel. On a day-to-day basis, and in the small details of everyday life, no doubt this is largely true. But in a deeper sense, all of us are enormously influenced by our personal histories. In particular, the circumstances and dynamics of our families exert a powerful effect on our later life. This is true whether we are conscious of it or not.

When a therapist takes a patient's history, he or she is not only interested in the details, but in the patterns that may have been unconsciously learned. For example, Carol's acceptance of mistreatment and inability to assert her own needs were baffling behaviors for such a capable and accomplished person. They only made sense when you consider her family history: both she and her mother were completely dominated by her self-absorbed father. She wasn't permitted to express her dissatisfaction; in fact she couldn't even remember that she was mistreated. Instead she transformed the experience into a fantasy, idealized relationship in order to make it tolerable. No wonder her relationships as an adult were so abusive and self-denying. That pattern couldn't change until she could remember it more accurately- with the slow, encouraging support of the psychotherapy relationship.

3. **The relationship between therapist and patient provides a major opportunity for reworking and healing old emotional wounds.**

Psychotherapy is a very intimate process. Because the therapist and patient are discussing such deeply emotional issues, it is inevitable that strong feelings, both positive as well as negative, will be stirred up in relation to the therapist. This is not an impediment to the work; indeed it often takes the work to a deeper level. Many unconscious feelings towards family members or authority figures that may have been repressed can be evoked and transferred onto the therapist. The therapist is always alert to the possibility that this is happening, and pays particular attention to shifts in attitude, behavior, or emotional tone that might signal such a process.

For example, a patient whose mother was experienced as critical and controlling may begin to make cutting, sarcastic comments towards his therapist, or question her commitment or interest in him. He starts showing up late for his appointments, or forgets an appointment and then complains about being charged for the missed session. Rather than being offended, the therapist begins to see that these are feelings that perhaps were meant to be directed at the patient's mother, but could not be spoken directly to her. In bringing this to the patient's attention, tactfully and without defensiveness, she may be able to help the patient explore more deeply how wounded he felt by his mother's hurtful comments. Furthermore, he may then be able to recognize that some of the people he becomes angry or annoyed with in his daily life are not really deserving of such treatment; they are also substitutes for his mother.

4. Psychotherapy focuses on the patient, not the diagnosis.

When we think of going to a physician, usually we are suffering from a particular disorder with a defined set of symptoms: fever, rash, swollen tissue, bodily pain. Our expectation is that the doctor will diagnose the condition and then prescribe a specific regimen or medication directly related to that symptom pattern. The doctor's skill lies chiefly in his or her ability to arrive at an accurate diagnosis. Once that is done, treatment follows a relatively standardized course, which is derived from relevant clinical studies.

For most psychological issues, the process is quite different. Unlike most medical procedures, psychotherapy is not standardized, nor could it be. The focus is on the patient's very particular and unique personality and how his or her problems and symptoms are related to underlying, usually unconscious processes. The patient's symptoms are often not the most important focus; nor is the diagnosis the most crucial step in determining the treatment. Rather, what matters most is the skill of the therapist in understanding who the patient is, and how to establish a strong working relationship with him or her. This relationship is crucial. Only in the context of the supportive emotional environment that the therapist creates can the patient be guided through the difficult task of challenging old assumptions and confronting deep-seated fears.

5. **The course of any given patient's psychotherapy is unpredictable and fluid. It changes as the therapist understands more about the patient, and it may have unexpected ups and downs.**

Precisely because psychotherapy focuses on the person, not the symptoms, it requires deep understanding of the patient's thoughts, feelings, memories, and relationships. This is a very complex undertaking. Patients cannot tell the therapist exactly what is wrong or how to make sense of their sometimes irrational behavior; more often than not, the patient doesn't know. At first, the therapist doesn't know either. The only way for the therapist to know what the patient's true problems are is to listen very carefully with a professionally trained eye and ear. In the case of Jimmy, he was completely bewildered by his sudden depression. He didn't explain where it came from or what it meant, because he had no idea. It was only by appreciating who he was, hearing his history, seeing how he behaved and what he was reacting to emotionally that I came to understand his depression and how to heal it.

Even when the therapist begins to understand the patient's underlying dynamics, there are often unforeseen shifts in focus or interaction that may change the course of the therapy. It is not uncommon after a period of time to hit a sort of plateau where little seems to be happening, or where the patient begins to express discomfort or irritation with the process. An experienced therapist does not take these changes at face value or become discouraged. Rather, he or she begins to look at what may be stirred up that is causing this shift in productivity or emotion. Often, this change signals the presence of deeply troubling memories or feelings that the patient is trying to suppress. If the therapist does not handle this crisis sensitively, the patient may terminate abruptly in order to avoid intolerable emotional pain. The patient needs the therapist to have the confidence and skill to tolerate

1. UNDERSTANDING THE PROCESS

the patient's unhappiness or discomfort. In doing so, the patient is empowered to tolerate it as well.

6. **The pace of the treatment is determined more by the complexity of the patient's emotional defenses than by the skill of the therapist.**

No matter how skilled the therapist may be, psychotherapy that deals with complex and fundamental emotional issues can only proceed as quickly as the patient can tolerate. This may seem odd. Doesn't the patient want to get better as quickly as possible? And shouldn't more experienced or skilled practitioners be able to achieve results more quickly? These are reasonable assumptions, but they don't reflect how psychotherapy actually works. Treatment is not teaching or explaining; it is more like exploration and reconstruction. What must be explored is mostly unconscious, so there is no direct pathway to understanding the patient's underlying conflicts. The therapist must deduce and infer what is happening, rather than observing the problem directly.

Furthermore, there are usually reasons why the patient's difficulties require more than simple problem-solving. Most often, it is because the patient is struggling with painful or shameful feelings that he or she is trying to manage by keeping them out of conscious awareness. This type of self-protective "not knowing" process occurs through *defense mechanisms*. We encountered these in the two case studies. For Jimmy, painful thoughts were projected, that is, he unconsciously warded them off by having other people feel them, rather than experience them himself. For Carol, disturbing experiences were kept out of awareness through denial, a defense which converts a disturbing feeling or memory into more palatable form. These are only two of the many complicated ways that we protect ourselves from emotional pain. The more a patient relies on these defense mechanisms for protection, the more difficult it becomes to understand what lies underneath them. Neither patient nor therapist can bulldoze through or circumvent them. Only when the patient has begun to feel that he or she can risk letting go of these protective distortions can the therapist unearth the patient's deeper feelings. A large part of the therapist's skill lies in knowing how to read when the patient is ready to take that step. The process cannot be rushed

7. **Over time, the insights and changes in self-awareness that are experienced in the psychotherapy sessions become part of the patient's daily life.**

Despite the intense interest in the historical roots of the patient's problems, psychotherapy's focus is actually more on the present and the future. Within the sessions, both patient and therapist need to be very in-the-moment. The patient is focused on saying whatever is of most interest or urgency at that moment, while the therapist listens and watches carefully. Both are reflecting on the emotions that are stirred up, where the patient becomes blocked, what is remembered, what is forgotten, slips of the tongue, shifts in the interaction between them: all of the clues that help the patient understand him or herself better.

As the process proceeds, usually patients will begin to notice changes in behavior outside of the therapy office as well. A situation that usually would have made them feel angry or hurt or anxious is experienced without those emotions. Or they were surprised to see themselves acting very differently than they usually did with an important person in their life. These experiences, in turn, become the object of reflection and further analysis within the therapy process. The changes occurring outside the office are connected up with changes occurring in the therapy. Gradually, the patient becomes aware not only of what is changing, but why and how. *"I was able to confront my husband about interrupting me, because I no longer felt so afraid that he would reject me, the way my brother always did."* Or *" I was able to take an airplane trip for the first time in years, because I no longer felt that I had to be in total control of everything all the time, as I had to be in my chaotic family. I could actually trust that it wouldn't be disastrous if I let someone else do something for me."*

As these changes in functioning and feeling accumulate, much of the urgency for being in therapy diminishes. Sometimes this allows the patient to focus on other important issues that had been neglected. But often, as the patient begins to feel consistently happier and more functional, there is less and less to say. This is a signal that the therapy is coming to a successful end. Either patient or therapist may suggest termination at this point; frequently they both feel the end coming about the same time. Ideally, once termination has been agreed upon, time will be taken to reflect on what has been accomplished and how the patient feels about the experience. Then patient and therapist say their goodbyes, knowing that the patient can return if he or she ever needs to, but that it is entirely possible they may never meet again.

For some time after terminating therapy, there is an internal consolidation of the process within the patient's mind. He or she may actually hear the therapist's voice, or remember something the therapist said about a particular issue. Gradually, these thoughts become less prominent. The therapist, once so prominent in the patient's life, fades into the background as the patient integrates all that he or she has learned into the flow of daily living. The therapy is now completed.

2. MEDICINE, PSYCHOLOGY AND THE PROBLEM OF DIAGNOSIS

In the last chapter, I stated that in psychotherapy, diagnosis matters far less than in medicine. This does not mean that the patient's diagnosis is immaterial. But diagnosis means something very different for psychotherapists. For the physician, the key question is *what is the illness?* But the psychotherapist is more interested in knowing *who is this person?* These differences between physicians and psychotherapists are not just stylistic, but reflect fundamentally different processes and objectives. Physicians live in a world of sophisticated technology, lab tests, pharmaceuticals, and diagnostic procedures that are linked to standardized treatments. Patients are usually seen sporadically during a medical crisis or an acute flare-up of a chronic ailment. Appointments tend to be brief, and are focused on diagnosing and treating a disease. The doctor generally knows very little about the patient's personal life, except for risk factors related to his or her physical health.

Psychotherapists, on the other hand, are mostly focused on very intimate details of their patients' lives. It's a decidedly non-technical world with deliberately non-standardized treatments that are provided at regular intervals, often for long periods of time. With the exception of the minority of psychiatrists who both prescribe medication and provide psychotherapy (currently less than 15% of psychiatrists), psychotherapists' medical expertise is mostly confined to knowledge of neuroanatomy and familiarity with psychiatric drugs.

For the physician, precise diagnosis is critical, because it directly determines the treatment protocol. A painful, persistent headache could be due to sinusitis, or it could be a sign of a brain tumor. In many cases, it doesn't much matter how well the physician knows the patient; what matters is that the disease is correctly diagnosed. Symptom patterns reveal the diagnosis, and the diagnosis directs the treatment. This is generally not the case in psychotherapy, where what matters most is not the nature of the disease but the nature of the person coming in for treatment. True, most patients will complain of certain symptoms, such as anxiety or depression. But these symptoms don't reveal that much; context, history, and personality structure are the keys to understanding the patient, and tell the therapist what to focus on and what kind of treatment is likely to be most effective.

When psychotherapists don't look beyond the patient's presenting symptoms or cling to a diagnostic label, the patient is likely to be misunderstood. This can lead to improper or ineffective treatment, as demonstrated in the cases below.

KYLE: A CASE OF MISDIAGNOSIS

I was about the sixth psychologist Kyle had seen, not counting the innumerable psychiatrists he had seen for medication. As usual, he was asking for help because of constant depression. He felt sad, lethargic, slept most of the time, was barely able to function at work, and was increasingly isolated from friends and family. Although he was on both an anti-depressant and a mood stabilizing agent, he was getting no relief from these medications. A friend of his had worked with me several years earlier, and suggested that I could help him. So Kyle called, wondering if perhaps this time would be different.

I wondered too. How could it possibly be that of all the therapists and psychiatrists he'd seen, none had been able to help him? I took a very careful history, including not only his family background, school, friendships and work, but of all of the prior treatment experiences, and what had gone wrong. I began to understand why he never improved: the diagnosis was wrong. He was not depressed.

2. MEDICINE, PSYCHOLOGY AND THE PROBLEM OF DIAGNOSIS

No doubt this seems like an odd statement. Kyle had every depressive symptom in the book. How could I say he was not depressed? My answer is that when examining psychological problems, symptoms should not be the only basis for a diagnosis. What matters far more is the underlying structure of the patient's personality. The same symptoms in a different personality can have a very different meaning. Kyle seemed depressed, and that is what he complained of. But his history and way of thinking revealed something more fundamental. All of his problems were blamed on someone or something beyond himself, often with an angry accusatory tone. His relationships, including with psychotherapists nearly always ended because he felt he had been betrayed in some way. Of course it is profoundly depressing to live this way; but depression was not the correct diagnosis. The diagnosis was paranoia.

A patient with a paranoid personality disorder is not easy to treat. But it can be done, with the right approach. The first step was to get him on an appropriate medication. I referred Kyle to a psychiatrist colleague whom I knew to be an outstanding clinician. He came to the same conclusions as I had, and took him off all anti-depressants, prescribing an anti-psychotic medication instead. Within a few months, most of the depressive symptoms diminished. It was now possible to pursue psychotherapy, although the therapy was very slow and difficult. Kyle was suspicious of nearly everything I did, so I had to be explicit about what I was thinking and the basis for my comments and suggestions. I also told him that he could fire me at any time, as long as he gave me two weeks' notice. That amused him, but my intent was serious. With paranoid patients, trust is the essential issue. Accordingly, I wanted to make it clear that he was in control of the therapy process. This is not the kind of offer I would make to a depressed patient, because with depression, self-criticism, guilt, or abandonment are the more fundamental issues. But I was certain that paranoia was what I needed to address: his underlying personality structure was far more diagnostic than his seemingly depressive symptoms, which I essentially ignored. In the end, my approach worked. He stayed with the therapy for many years, and though he was never truly comfortable with people, he functioned much better and had no recurrence of the depressive symptoms that had plagued him for so long.

INSIDE YOUR THERAPIST'S MIND

TWO ALCOHOLIC PATIENTS, TWO DIFFERENT TREATMENTS

Several years ago, I had the experience of seeing two patients who had recently been discharged from the same alcoholism treatment center. Frank was a man in his mid-thirties, angry, belligerent, with a history of arrests for bar fights and drunk driving. Paula was a woman in her fifties, painfully shy and fearful, who seemed to be almost completely isolated from the world. These two patients had only one thing in common: neither had been able to stay sober for very long after their discharge from inpatient treatment. The problem, as I understood it, was that because they were both diagnosed as alcoholic, they had been given essentially identical treatment. It was no surprise therefore that they were drinking again. The rehab had focused only on their common disease, rather than on the person who had the disease. So the diagnosis was correct, but insufficient. The far more important diagnostic questions of their underlying personality structures and motivation were left entirely unexplored.

In order to treat these patients, I needed to spend time with them to understand the function of alcohol in their lives. Central to Frank's drinking was his resentment of authority, and his need to discharge his chronic anger at the world. His father had been very violent and abusive; though he resented him, Frank was unconsciously following right in his footsteps. When he drank, he looked for fights and for any external situation that to his mind would justify angry reprisals. It was very clear to me that given this dynamic, I couldn't be the primary engine of his recovery. He would end up seeing me as yet another male authority to defy. Instead, I focused on his resistance to AA, which I saw as a potentially less threatening source of guidance and constructive confrontation for him. Whenever he complained of the "know-it-all" guys who turned him off at the meetings, I suggested he find a more congenial group or focus instead on the lower-key people he did like. I downplayed my role or advice, suggesting to him that other people in his situation would understand him better than I. He ultimately did start hanging out with a group of young men in AA whose advice he

2. MEDICINE, PSYCHOLOGY AND THE PROBLEM OF DIAGNOSIS

could accept without resentment. The fact that he kept coming to his appointments with me meant that he clearly knew that I was helpful to him, but I downplayed my role, and instead reinforced his relationship with these other young men.

As a result of this approach, Frank had time to consolidate his sobriety, anchored in relationships that did not threaten him. My patience with him allowed him to slowly, and subconsciously, experience me as someone whose counsel he could also accept. It was only then that we talked explicitly about his underlying issues with his father: how his feelings about him were connected to his self-destructiveness and aggressive acting out, including his drinking. Sobriety became for him not something he had to do, but something he wanted to do, as an expression of a strong, independent identity.

Paula's issues were quite different, which required a very different approach. She had grown up in a large family, with parents who were so emotionally and financially overwhelmed that no one got very much time or attention. For some of the children, who were either very talented or outgoing, there were alternate sources of attention. But for Paula, who seems to have been a very sensitive, introverted child, there was nothing but pain. She was awkward, very shy, lacking in confidence, and hypersensitive to criticism or rejection. People were never a source of comfort; they were a problem to be avoided. Drinking was something she discovered in college, as a way to dull her social anxiety and as she put it, "pass for normal." She never anticipated that this "solution" to her problem could become a problem of its own.

Unlike Frank, Paula was not opposed to AA, but it was simply too overwhelming for her to be open, or even to be in the presence of so many other people. She could, however, tolerate talking to me. She was clearly drawing comfort from experiencing me as someone who was interested in her as a person, and sympathetic to her problems. We spent two years exploring her suffering in childhood and adolescence. She began to understand why she had put her faith in alcohol, rather than in people. Only when I sensed that she could trust my support implicitly did I begin to encourage her to attend AA. But, as one would expect, it was far from easy for her. I had to help her interpret other members' responses to her, help her see that they shared many of her feelings and could really empathize with her. Very gradually and tentatively, she began to see herself as part of a group of other people. It was not just about abstinence; it was about joining the world for the first time.

These cases are not about the incompetence of previous practitioners. The diagnoses they arrived at were plausible and partly correct, based on the patients' symptoms. However, the diagnoses were derived from a medical, rather than a psychological process. The patients were found to have a disease, depression or alcoholism, and then standard procedures were employed to treat that disease. With primarily medical disorders, that would be good practice. But for psychological disorders, a medical diagnosis misses the point. Psychological diagnosis is not symptom focused. The patient's symptoms have to be decoded to understand what lies beneath them - to understand who the person is, and what his or her true problems are. The person, not the disease, is the focus. That is the essence of psychotherapy, and what distinguishes it from medical treatment.

DIAGNOSTIC OVERSIMPLIFICATION: THE PROBLEM OF PSEUDO-SCIENCE

Confusing psychology and medicine is one source of diagnostic problems. But there is yet another. Increasingly, psychologists and other mental health professionals are being encouraged to justify their diagnostic and treatment decisions as "empirically validated." What this means is that the data used for making diagnostic decisions must be more "objective" and therefore more like chemistry, physics, and other hard sciences. If the behaviors are not directly observable, they are not considered "scientific," and therefore not valid.

The problem with this diagnostic approach is that it assumes that studying physical phenomena and psychological processes are essentially similar, and can utilize the same scientific methodology. But psychology is not physics. It is a human science, where the data of importance involve phenomena that are not always directly observable.

2. MEDICINE, PSYCHOLOGY AND THE PROBLEM OF DIAGNOSIS

Psychological diagnosis, when properly done, requires a great deal of skill and inference. Under the misguided notions of evidence-based practice, looking beneath the surface of a patient's behavior, including intuition, clinical experience or interpretation becomes suspect, because these are not objective measures that nearly every observer could agree upon. As a result, psycho-diagnosis has been transformed from a discipline that involves a complex weighing of many kinds of objective and subjective observation to a mechanical procedure that only values the cataloguing of symptoms. This virtually ensures that diagnosing a patient's condition will either be superficial or grossly inaccurate.

Adding to this confusion is another bit of pseudo-science: the insistence that psychological disorders be classified as a subcategory of diseases, much like other medical disorders. In fact, with the exception of a few very severe illnesses such as schizophrenia and bipolar disorder, most psychological disturbances reflect behavioral patterns that result from traumatic experiences which distort the patient's intellectual and emotional functioning in very complicated ways. There may well be physiological changes that accompany the emotional and cognitive disturbance. Nevertheless, they cannot realistically be understood as diseases at all. This demand that psychological problems be viewed as medical diseases may have seemed at one time to be an enlightened view. After all, it is far less stigmatizing to have a disease for which one cannot be blamed than to have an emotional problem or "weakness." But it is far better to recognize this stigmatization as an unfounded prejudice than to create a medical fiction.

Three factors in particular have accelerated this distorted state of affairs. The first factor, which in turn has greatly influenced the other two, is the almost complete dominance of the medical field by health insurance. Nearly all health care services are now paid, partly or entirely, by either government-sponsored or private insurance. Effectively, this means that as a practical matter, disorders exist if the insurance company who pays the bills decides they exist. Theoretically, they can say they are not making such judgments as they have no wish to encroach upon the doctor's expertise and professional prerogatives. "Talk to your doctor..." as the pharmaceutical commercials are always careful to state. But the doctor knows who pays the bill, and what disorders will not be reimbursed.

As a society, we have made a devil's bargain with the insurance companies. Both patients and providers want to feel that nothing will intrude upon the sacred doctor-patient relationship. We just want the insurance company to help pay the bills. So it seems, at first, like a small thing to adjust procedures or diagnostic coding to conform to insurance requirements. However, these small adjustments accumulate; what starts out as a bureaucratic procedure subliminally becomes the conventional way of thinking. In diagnostics, this often means that the definition of a particular disorder is stretched beyond reasonable limits, and this expansion is rationalized by the provider. An unreimbursable condition begins to disappear, as it is merged into a diagnostic category that literally "fits the bill." Doctors and insurance companies can continue to claim that the doctor's judgment and authority have not been unduly influenced, but as if by magic, diagnoses move in the direction of payment.

A second contributing factor is the emergence of the well-known Diagnostic and Statistical Manual (DSM) as the authoritative source for determining psychiatric diagnoses. In its earliest form in the 1960s, the DSM contained complex diagnostic categories that required that the diagnostician had a deep knowledge of the formation and development of personality traits and of the complex processes that work beneath the surface of a patient's symptoms. It was assumed that a clinician needed to have a very sophisticated understanding of emotional development and psychopathology to make an informed diagnosis. But the publishers of the DSM, the American Psychiatric Association, became alarmed at the finding that the degree of agreement between clinicians for a given diagnosis was surprisingly low. How could they claim that psycho-diagnosis was a scientifically valid procedure if so few clinicians came up with the same diagnosis for the same patient? There were two obvious solutions to this problem. The first would be better training, to ensure that clinicians were sufficiently versed in the subtleties of personality development to make more sophisticated diagnostic judgments. The other would be to simplify the diagnostic categories so that such specialized knowledge would be unnecessary.

2. MEDICINE, PSYCHOLOGY AND THE PROBLEM OF DIAGNOSIS

The publishers chose the latter course. Beginning with the third edition (DSM-III), psycho-diagnosis became accessible to all. It was so accessible, in fact, that it soon became one of the county's best-selling reference books. Anyone can now go to Barnes and Noble or Amazon, buy the DSM-IV and by following the menus laid out in the book, make the same diagnosis as their doctor. It all seems fairly easy, and it is if all that matters are observable symptoms.

The third great amplifier of distortion in psycho-diagnostics comes from the over-reliance on psychiatric medications in medicine and psychiatry. Beginning in the 1980s, the large pharmaceutical corporations developed a new class of anti-depressants known as SSRIs which had far fewer side-effects than the older medications. We are all familiar with these drugs: Prozac, Zoloft, Paxil, and more recently, Celexa and Lexapro. Your physician is even more familiar with them, because he or she has been targeted by pharmaceutical companies to recommend these products. This marketing alone would probably not be enough to have convinced them to use these medications, however. Physicians are highly motivated to do good; they need evidence to convince them that new products can help to ease their patients' ailments. Armed with scores of clinical trials in medical journals that demonstrated impressive rates of response to these new drugs, physicians were reassured that depression, in particular, could now be easily treated pharmacologically. Unfortunately, it took nearly two decades for much of this research to be questioned. When the drug trials for these medications were later re-analyzed by the Food and Drug Administration, it was discovered that many of the pharmaceutical manufacturers had failed to report those clinical trials that did not confirm their product's efficacy. When the full data base was then evaluated, the effectiveness of these newer anti-depressants was shown to be far less than had been claimed earlier. They were most effective with severe depression; with milder depression, these medications performed only slightly better than placebo. So they were not miracle drugs after all, just one of many potential treatment tools.

But by the time these later findings were reported, these medications had become the standard treatment. Physicians, even those without specialized psychiatric training came to believe that depressive symptoms could be matched to a specifically targeted medication and be effectively treated. If a patient came into a physician's office complaining of sadness, unexplained crying spells, nervousness, or loss of appetite, it was possible to write a prescription for one of these drugs and hope that the symptoms improved. Often enough, they did, at least for the short follow-up period typical in a busy internist or family practitioner's practice. It was therefore assumed that the diagnosis, arrived at without special expertise, was correct.

At the same time, the training of psychiatrists, who for so long had been deeply trained in diagnostics, psychotherapy, and psycho-pharmacology, became almost exclusively about which drug to prescribe for what condition. I think this was not just a response to pharmaceutical marketing, but a deeper, more fundamental problem of professional identity. As we have seen, psychological problems require a different diagnostic approach than is used for medical disorders. For this very reason, psychiatry has always held a precarious position in the medical profession. Freud himself was never fully accepted by the medical community in his lifetime. Though he had been a highly regarded neurologist, once he turned his attention to psychology and psychoanalysis, his medical colleagues in Vienna generally shunned him. To them, he was no longer a real doctor, but an unscientific crackpot.

In this country, psychiatrists had similarly been unfairly relegated to the bottom of the medical profession's hierarchy in terms of income and esteem by other physicians. But beginning in the 1970s, the psychiatric profession began a concerted focus on the physiological and medical basis of psychiatric disorders. This was framed as a scientific undertaking, but I believe it was mostly an exercise in identity and self-esteem. With this shift in focus, psychiatrists could align themselves with "real doctors," and perhaps increase their professional standing. This also allowed them to differentiate themselves from non-physician psychotherapists. (Non-physicians cannot prescribe; psychiatrists are the only mental health specialists who can). So psychiatrists, in effect, became "brain scientists," interpreting emotional and behavioral problems as medical illnesses that required medical treatments, most notably medication. The diagnosis was linked to the drug. Conditions that could not reliably be treated with medications stopped being

2. MEDICINE, PSYCHOLOGY AND THE PROBLEM OF DIAGNOSIS

diagnosed, while those conditions that were thought to be responsive to medication become over-diagnosed.

Matching patient symptoms to a manual or medication is not science; it is pseudo-science. Only in textbooks do psychiatric patients come in with clearly defined illnesses that can be remedied by a specific, targeted treatment. In actual practice, when a patient contacts a psychotherapist, his or her symptoms are likely to be vague or to reflect multiple problems. Patients often cannot tell the therapist exactly what is wrong; they don't know, because the causes of their distress are often unconscious. An experienced clinician understands this and therefore doesn't take the initial presentation at face value. He or she wants to know more about the patient than just the symptoms; what matters is the entire context of the person's life. Assigning a scientific-sounding diagnostic label or immediately prescribing a palliative medication places the emphasis on the disease rather than on the patient. It is dismissive, superficial, and more often than not, produces incorrect or meaningless diagnoses.

The true diagnostic question that faces every psychotherapist is simply this: who is this person, and what is the meaning of her or his suffering? Every patient comes in with pathological symptoms. These can include such wide-ranging issues as anxiety, sadness, chronic anger, sleep problems, relationship difficulties, addictions to various substances, compulsive behaviors, unwanted thoughts, chronic pain or fatigue, or combinations of many of the above. Anyone, including the patient, can catalogue the symptoms and come up with a diagnosis that matches the particular pattern they exhibit. But it doesn't help much. Patients need someone to think about what these symptoms mean in the context of who they are, and what their history has been. This takes training, self-awareness, and talent on the part of the therapist. Accuracy in psycho-diagnosis, and ultimately appropriate treatment, thus relies almost entirely upon the complex abilities of the psychotherapist. We must therefore now turn to the making of a psychotherapist, upon whom so much depends.

3. THE MAKING OF A PSYCHOTHERAPIST

Most of us have had the experience of reading a passage in a book that was so well-written that it seemed to flow effortlessly from the author. Only upon reflection do we realize that it could not have been so; the elegance and efficiency of the passage obscures the difficulty of creating it. This is what good psychotherapy is often like. Comments or interventions that seem casual are not. When therapists do their job well, the careful calculations about what each particular patient's issues are, what they need at that moment, and how to best communicate with them are made very quickly, often without any evidence of effort.

Let me give you an example of what I mean. Not long ago, I was working with a young woman who was severely depressed. We spent several months going over her current problems as well as how they might connect to her life history. As often happens, she began to feel a sense of relief just by unburdening herself of the lonely, isolating feeling of being trapped in her despair. But as we began to talk more about her current circumstances, her mood darkened and progress stopped. Increasingly, all she could talk about was her marriage. Her husband, whom she had always seen as a supportive presence, had begun criticizing her for her constant "bad moods." He saw her as weak and self-indulgent, and was particularly annoyed that she was often not interested in sex.

It became clear to me that we would have to address the conflicts with her husband in order to be able to treat her depression. I suggested that perhaps they might consider a referral for couples therapy. When she discussed this with her husband, he was dismissive of the suggestion. But, surprisingly, he did say that he wouldn't mind talking to someone himself, because he was getting so frustrated with the situation and needed some "coping tools." She asked for a referral for him, and I promptly provided the name of a colleague whom I thought might be a good fit.

Nothing much changed for several months, except that the husband had begun seeing the therapist I recommended. But gradually, my patient began to feel less hopeless. Her husband's tone was softer, he was more patient with her, and she was beginning to have more periods in her life where she felt good about herself. Without the constant conflict at home, she was now much more able to concentrate on her internal conflicts which were so clearly connected to her history of depression throughout her life. Our work was going well, and she began to see the relationship between her thoughts, feelings, and past experiences which kept her so unhappy.

At first glance, this case example might seem to be utterly mundane: a patient needed a referral so I made one, and it worked out. But it actually reflected a number of subtle, but essential processes. Embedded in this case were dozens of complex assessments and interventions that I made, each of which contributed to the positive changes experienced by the patient. Though they flowed organically within the therapy sessions, these decisions can be broken down separately for purposes of instruction:

1. I saw that the patient was quite depressed, but able to talk freely. At the same time, I felt calm, pleased to see her, and able to think clearly when I was in session with her. These were good signs, because it meant that this was a person who was truly open to the help that psychotherapy could provide. I knew this both intellectually and emotionally, by monitoring my own experiences when I was with her.

3. THE MAKING OF A PSYCHOTHERAPIST

2. Knowing that she was open to self-reflection allowed me to see that when she switched from talking mostly about herself to her marital relationship, that this was not just defensive or avoidant. It wasn't that she didn't want to focus on herself. It was that something about her relationship with her husband was interfering with the process.

3. The timing of her husband's increasing negativity was informative. She had been depressed for quite some time, but had generally found her husband supportive of her. His increasing negativity did not begin until after she began psychotherapy. This signaled that her involvement in therapy and perhaps her involvement with me in particular, were experienced by him as a threat.

4. Suggesting couples therapy at this point had two benefits. First, if they accepted the referral, the husband's interference with her treatment could be minimized. Secondly, even if he was unwilling to go to couples therapy, it would subconsciously convey my confidence in her. It said, in effect, that I believe what you are telling me about the problems you are having with him. And further, I believe that the difficulties you are having in therapy now are not because you are unable or unwilling to get better. It is something outside of you.

5. Her husband's rejection of couples therapy told me that this was someone who was unwilling to consider that he was part of the problem. As far as he was concerned, his wife was the one with the problem, not he.

6. However, the husband's unsolicited suggestion that maybe he should see someone signaled subconscious awareness that indeed he did have a problem worth investigating. It didn't matter that he attributed this interest to needing to learn how to deal with her. I understood that as a defensive, face-saving way to get into therapy without having to formally admit that he needed it.

7. The therapist I referred him to was a man who I felt would intuitively understand the husband's personality and defenses. He would be

able to engage him in the process of looking at himself even though that was not at all what the husband was consciously planning as an objective.

8. This particular therapist was not someone I knew well. I knew only the general outlines of his training and areas of expertise. But I had spent several days with him at a professional conference, and I had a very good sense of him as a person, of the way he thought, how flexible and intuitive he was, and what kind of relationship he would build with this particular patient.

Of course, the positive outcome I've just described was not guaranteed to happen. Sometimes, despite your best judgment and skill, your work doesn't succeed. But each of the steps I took, the moment-to-moment assessments I made, increased the likelihood of success. What happened reflected the complex interaction of professional knowledge, careful training, self-awareness, and the special personal attributes and intuitive gifts that all competent psychotherapists must have. In order to better understand the role of these components, it will be necessary to examine each of them in more detail.

PROFESSIONAL KNOWLEDGE

What kind of knowledge base is necessary for a therapist to be competent? The short answer would be this: everything essential about human behavior and motivation. It is not too much to expect a psychotherapist who is entrusted with the care of patients to have a comprehensive understanding of human behavior. At a minimum, this should include the following components:

1. A working knowledge of neuroanatomy, physiology, evolutionary biology, and symptoms of brain dysfunction.

2. A thorough grounding in developmental psychology. This entails understanding the sequence and processes involved in the

3. THE MAKING OF A PSYCHOTHERAPIST

maturation of the individual from infancy through adulthood, as well as recognition of the significant issues and crises of each stage of life.

3. A deep knowledge of marital and family dynamics; how families function and how dysfunctions may occur.

4. A comprehensive understanding of personality structure and personality types, both normal and abnormal.

5. Familiarity with the full range of psychiatric disorders and skill at differential diagnosis.

6. Familiarity with a wide range of approaches to psychotherapy, including not just different conceptual systems (for example cognitive-behavioral vs. psychodynamic vs. interpersonal) but different modalities (individual, couples, family, or group).

Acquiring each of these skill sets requires both academic study and clinical training. The classroom can only prepare a clinician so far; he or she must then translate this intellectual knowledge into recognition and understanding of how these phenomena occur in therapeutic encounters with patients. This is accomplished through careful supervision by well-trained, experienced mentors. This process involves not strictly intellectual, but emotional and interpersonal learning. Within the bounds of mutual respect and empathy for all the difficulties involved in experiential learning, the supervisor must question and challenge the novice psychotherapist to explain every clinical hypothesis, thought, or feeling that is experienced, as well as every comment, and intervention he or she makes in the course of a therapy session. The supervisor wants to inculcate the habit of constant self-reflection, attending to all of the mental, physical, and emotional cues that arise in the course of a therapy session. Only when the developing therapist has internalized this process of constant inquiry and observation is he or she ready to assume the complex, constantly challenging work of treating patients.

I have very vivid memories of how emotionally taxing this kind of learning can be. In one of my most difficult experiences during my internship at a university medical center, I was assigned an adolescent girl who had been admitted to the psychiatric ward because of a serious suicide attempt. She was a very angry and rebellious girl, whose hostility masked profound depression, identity confusion, and severe family dysfunction. Things went well enough at first. I met with her for an initial evaluation, took some history, and began the process of initiating therapy. But by our third individual session, she refused to talk to me. I was extremely uncomfortable with this, especially in a hospital setting where one's work is very public: every staff member knows something about what is going on with every patient on the unit. What I most feared was being seen as incompetent. I wanted to hand off the care of this patient to someone else, since it seemed obvious that everyone could see that she was uncomfortable with me. My supervisor insisted that my fears had more to do with my own insecurities than with whether she was receiving adequate treatment. We focused more upon what was being stirred up in me by her behavior than on her behavior itself. It was only because I was forced to look at my own feelings and experience that I began to learn that the therapy was far more productive than I could have imagined. The feelings of shame, incompetence, and paralysis were hers; that's what she was trying to tell me. I had to accept and learn how to interpret her projection of these feelings onto me. This required me to show up every day, for every session, whether she talked or not, or even showed up for the appointment. What mattered was that I took her seriously, that I kept my commitment, and that she was free to communicate, in whatever way she could, just how hurt she felt. And surprisingly, she made very good progress. By the end of her stay in the psychiatric ward, she was far less angry, not suicidal, and had been able to start talking to her parents about how she felt. After our last session, again without any words spoken by her, she left my office, grabbed hold of an old man who was a fellow patient, and hugged him for several minutes. By then, I had learned to read her non-verbal communications.

3. THE MAKING OF A PSYCHOTHERAPIST

SELF-AWARENESS: THE PSYCHOTHERAPIST'S PERSONAL THERAPY

I was 22 at the time, midway through my first year in graduate school. I had just begun seeing my therapist, a psychiatrist who had also been trained as a psychoanalyst. He knew my basic issues, something about my family background, and that I was looking for help with anxiety. At the beginning of the third session, he invited me to lie on the couch. How quaint, I thought, just like a New Yorker cartoon: the patient lies on the couch and free associates while the analyst listens, maybe speaking a few sage lines at the end. So without hesitation, I lay down, expecting this to be a very routine process. That was not what happened. Within moments, my heart was pounding, and I was flooded with anxiety. I felt exposed, vulnerable, afraid of being hurt, afraid he would physically attack me. Though this went on for nearly 45 minutes, he said little, except to ask a few questions about what I was referring to or what I meant. And yet, his presence was reassuring. At the end of the hour, I sat up, drained but somehow relieved, and made a joke about how all this psychoanalytic stuff was a bunch of nonsense. We both laughed. Then we arranged to meet twice weekly, with each session on the couch. I did this for many years, supplemented eventually by once weekly group therapy sessions.

There were many more surprises to come. I had initiated psychotherapy because I was feeling extremely anxious and insecure in school. It wasn't that I wasn't bright enough, but I could see that I was feeling defensive and competitive with my classmates, and intimidated by my professors. What I didn't know was that this defensiveness and fear was not just situational. It was essential to my personality structure, formed by growing up in a violent, humiliating family where no one was ever safe.

I expected to come into therapy talking about how my childhood was basically fine, though tragically, my older sister committed suicide when I was 18. It was nobody's fault, I thought, just more of the troubles she'd always had with anger, acting out, and eventually, depression. All of that cover story began to collapse in therapy, beginning with the bodily sensations stirred up on the couch where I could literally feel the fear of being attacked. It wasn't immediately obvious to me what that had meant. But over time, I came to understand in an unmistakable way that this feeling represented the deeper truth about my family. My father was a tyrant, who intimidated all three children with his angry explosions, sarcastic remarks, and periodic beatings which were mostly directed at my sister. What made things worse was that my mother did almost nothing to protect us or stop the verbal and physical abuse. At first, I rationalized that she also was a victim of my father's abuse. But that, too, was a convenient excuse. She was herself a very angry person, frustrated and unhappy with her life as a housewife and mother. My sister's unwillingness to "do as you're told" was an intolerable challenge to her authority. As hard as it was for me to admit, she passively sanctioned my sister's beatings. As for me and my younger brother, we were left to fend for ourselves in this hostile environment. I coped by becoming the "good child" who never did anything wrong and learned how to please everyone. My brother simply withdrew and kept his mouth shut.

Being good and pleasing everyone is not a strategy for a happy life. It is what a prisoner does to survive. But for a long time, I counted myself as the fortunate one in the family, who "hardly ever got beaten."(It is somewhat embarrassing to admit that's how I thought back then). Though I was not consciously aware of feeling inadequate, I was determined to show to the world, and myself, that I was normal and could be conventionally successful. I married young, more or less choosing the first girl who was interested in me. Never mind that we had very little in common, that she had a way of mocking me with little jokes, that in fact, most of our conversations were basically small talk and logistical plans. I was relieved and happy that someone wanted me. In any case, intimacy in a relationship was an experience I knew nothing about. It was enough for me that we never had loud arguments, that there were no angry or violent outbursts, and that we always seemed to get along just fine. I prided myself on how much more harmonious my family life seemed than the family I had grown up in.

3. THE MAKING OF A PSYCHOTHERAPIST

It took me many years to see through the rationalizations about my marriage. The first cracks in my denial came very unexpectedly. I was talking about my mother, how tense and removed she was. I had an insight about her seeming passivity. It really wasn't passive at all; it was passive-aggressive. She expressed her anger constantly, but indirectly: not helping, not offering words of support or encouragement, ridiculing anything that seemed weak or childish to her. I was finally beginning to understand the complex dynamics that made my family so unsafe. But during a particular session, my flow of thoughts about my mother was suddenly interrupted. I experienced the sensation of having to catch my breath as I realized: my wife is just like my mother. It was not true that our life was harmonious; all the fighting was done in a passive-aggressive way. Potential disagreements never got to the level of argument: all she had to do was criticize or ridicule me, and I would not fight back. I would do whatever was needed to keep the peace, just as I had done all my life in my family.

I would like to say that once I became more aware of the problems in my marriage that I started to address them with her. But I did not. Incredibly, I managed to discount my earlier insight about my mother and my wife. It was many years before I would actually even remember having had those thoughts. Instead, I focused on what was working in my life: I was less anxious, succeeding professionally, enjoying being a father. In terms of day-to-day functioning, my life worked. I remained unconscious of the lack of real intimacy in my marriage, of the growing emptiness and loneliness I felt. Saying this now, it seems unbelievable that I could have been in such denial. But not letting myself be aware of uncomfortable feelings was entirely natural to me; it was my oldest survival mode. I did not remember because I was not ready to accept the consequences of awareness.

It took me a very long time to come to terms with the emptiness of my marriage. This consciousness came very slowly, years after I had actually concluded my therapy. As I look back on it now, I can see that the self-awareness I had developed in psychotherapy was gradually helping me recognize things I had always ignored. I began to see how my wife would condescendingly dismiss my questioning anything about our relationship. She too was in denial, and ironically, I think this denial had once been a source of connection between us. But now it was an unbreachable wall. I could no longer dismiss how I felt, and the inability to talk, the passive-aggressive undermining, and the absence of a mature, intimate connection eventually led to divorce. The tumultuousness of that change, along with many other unfinished issues that I had not understood also led me to resume psychotherapy.

There were, of course many more revelations to come in my subsequent therapy, beyond what I can convey here. For now, I think it is sufficient to comment on what my experience tells us about what role personal therapy plays in the training of the psychotherapist. To begin with, lets address the misconception that requiring therapists to have substantial therapy themselves is an outmoded vestige of Freudian analysis, and therefore unnecessary. This requirement may have started with psychoanalysis, but it applies to any serious therapy, of any theoretical school. Why? Because counseling and therapy requires extensive self-knowledge. Anyone can give advice, which is often useless because the advice-giver is mostly talking about superficial problem-solving. What makes a therapist's comment worthwhile is that it reflects an understanding that the problems we encounter in life are often more complex and irrational than we suppose. When therapists examine their own lives, they learn first-hand how vulnerable we all are to unconscious forces from our past. Supervision and reading alone cannot provide this awareness; it is acquired primarily by being a patient yourself.

Secondly, a therapist cannot take a patient to where he or she has never been. Therapists must know not only what needs to be looked at or questioned but how it feels to do so. Our impediments to understanding are most often not conceptual, but emotional. The therapist must empathically understand the pain that can be aroused in therapy, the patient's need to distort awareness to protect him or herself emotionally, and have compassion for the suffering and the courage involved in addressing one's problems. This intimate knowledge can come only from direct experience.

A third reason is that most psychotherapists, whether consciously or unconsciously, chose to be in the profession because of their own personal problems. In and of itself this is not problematic. Indeed, it

3. THE MAKING OF A PSYCHOTHERAPIST

probably could not be otherwise; it would be hard to sympathize and have the patience necessary to listen to others' problems if this were not intensely interesting to the therapist. This interest comes from the therapist's ability to identify with the patient's experience. But therapists must do more than identify with their patients. Those who do not also heal their own problems have innumerable blind spots that not only hinder treatment, but cause real harm. If a patient were to stir up disturbing issues that the therapist had not dealt with adequately, the therapist's own defenses would likely be activated. This defensive process might make the therapist feel better, but it would be an absolute disservice to the patient.

For psychotherapists, their own deep experience as a therapy patient is both humbling and necessary. Psychotherapists are not fundamentally different from their patients; they certainly are not smarter, morally superior, or inherently wiser. They gain their stature, and their credibility as healing professionals because they have grappled with many of the same traumas, failures, and disappointments, and used that personal motivation to not only heal themselves but to learn how to heal others.

TALENT AND TEMPERAMENT

Earlier in this chapter, I talked about referring my patient's husband to a therapist I trusted, but did not know well. What I did know about this therapist was that he possessed the temperament and intuitive gifts that the best psychotherapists all have. As it turned out, my judgment of him was correct; I suppose this speaks to my intuitive gifts as well. But what was it, exactly, that allowed me to make this judgment?

This is harder to convey than the other aspects of training we have discussed so far. Something more than professional training and even personal psychotherapy is required to produce the best practitioners; competent psychotherapists must possess a certain kind of gift to truly attune to their patients. Without this gift, the work is mechanical and by-the book. With it, the care can be individualized to each particular patient, allowing for transformational changes that would not be possible otherwise.

Musical performance provides a close analog to this kind of intangible quality. For example, musical compositions are written out so that any trained person who works with sufficient effort can play a tune more or less adequately. But a true musician adds something else; a feeling for the music that cannot be specified by the composer. The musician must feel it with a certain kind of intuitive understanding to go beyond mere mechanical reproduction. You can easily hear the difference between the two processes.

If you were to ask the best musicians how they made the music come alive, they would probably offer something about their knowledge of the composer, the musical era, or some technical detail of playing technique. None of these explanations would actually address what you've just heard. Somehow they intuitively understand the music and when you hear them play, you feel moved by what they've understood. What you've just experienced is the expression of talent.

This kind of gift is essential to being a competent psychotherapist. It comes in to play constantly, as early as the first appointment. For instance, during the initial interview, it is critically important for the therapist to both understand the true nature of the patient's difficulties and to communicate in such a way that the patient understands something they hadn't considered about what has gone wrong and what the treatment will entail. This is far harder than it looks. For one thing, patients' explanations of what is wrong are often only partially correct. They can only describe what they are aware of, not what they don't know. It is the therapist's job to listen for just these missing pieces. But even that is not sufficient. The therapist must also have a sense of *why* the particular patient doesn't understand more about his or her problem. In addition, the psychotherapist must listen carefully to how each patient thinks and speaks, in order to find a way to communicate with them in terms that will make sense, but will not be experienced as threatening or disrespectful. All of this must be done within the first hour. If not, it is likely the patient will either not return or fail to engage in the process.

3. THE MAKING OF A PSYCHOTHERAPIST

Very often, I will make an observation in the initial evaluation session, and hear the patient say to me "How did you know that?" At this point in my career, the simplest answer is to say "Well, I've been doing this for a long time." True enough, but my response actually begs the question. In fact, it is difficult to put into words. The precise kind of awareness that is required comes too quickly and in too much detail to be the product of ordinary thinking. Vast quantities of theoretical knowledge, clinical observation, and personal experience are rapidly combined, sorted, and processed. Often, much of this process is not even conscious. Yet before the hour is over, the skilled therapist will have formed an impression of the patient that is accurate enough that the patient resonates to the observation and feels deeply understood.

Something beyond training is going on here. This is not a technique, but the whole personality of the psychotherapist that makes these kinds of interactions possible. For the best therapists, there is something essential about them that makes them extraordinarily suited to the complex work of psychotherapy. I would characterize this personality as having the following components:

- A nearly limitless interest and fascination with people.
- An attuned ear and eye of such acuteness that both the prosaic and poetic elements of the patient are apprehended.
- An equally skillful use of language, to communicate these observations in a language that is both in sync with and intelligible to the patient.
- An ability to not only tolerate intimacy, but to cultivate it.
- A corresponding capacity to frame and maintain boundaries to protect both therapist and patient.
- Exceptional capacity for honesty, especially of the self-reflective, self-observing type.
- Abundant compassion, for self as well as others – so that both the patient's and therapist's mistakes can be tolerated, learning can be enjoyed, and failures or losses can be absorbed without shame or guilt.
- A strong sense of humor, which allows one to see the ironies of life without bitterness.

- Deep intuitive capacity, i.e., a particular kind of creative intelligence that allows one to go beyond mere facts to discover truth, even if it is only the patient's truth.
- Enthusiasm for life in all of its complexity, occasional perversity, and surprising moments of joy.
- Comfort with and humility in the use of one's own authority.

It is true that many of these personal qualities are only partly understandable as manifestations of talent. Certainly, you can see how training plays a role in the careful cultivation of these essential skills. But that is true of all of the separate forms of knowledge we've discussed. When skilled therapists treat their patients, they utilize a complex combination of academic training, clinical experience, personal awareness, and intuitive interpersonal skills to guide their work. It is seldom the case that only one of these inputs is relied upon to make the moment-to-moment judgments that shape each therapy session.

In a very real sense, then, the long process of training that produces a competent psychotherapist is not just about acquiring technical skills. It is always about developing a particular kind of person, who utilizes therapeutic skills derived from personal and professional knowledge. This is an important distinction. Knowledge alone does not heal people. Healing always takes place in the context of the relationship between two people: the doctor and patient. So we must now turn to the study of the unique interpersonal process of psychotherapy, to understand how patients heal by resolving their conflicts within an emotionally attuned and supportive relationship.

4. THE PSYCHOTHERAPY RELATIONSHIP

Nate was an older man, who had been referred by the human resources department of his company because of persistent conflicts with subordinates. Several of the people he managed complained of feeling mistreated, constantly criticized, micromanaged, and belittled. Nate was shocked to hear from his superiors that he had an "attitude problem." As far as he knew, he was a consistently high-performing manager, whose only problem at work was being saddled with employees whose work ethic was not up to his standards. It was humiliating to him that the company couldn't see how hard he worked, and how much effort it took to meet such high levels of productivity. He only accepted the referral for therapy because his boss insisted he needed to learn how to work better with people.

When I first met with Nate, he was exceedingly polite and deferential. In fact, he was uncomfortably polite. I felt tense sitting with him, despite his smiles, careful attention to everything I said, and willingness to agree with my observations. The content of his speech could not have been more agreeable. But there was a kind of rigidity in his manner that felt frightening, as though some seething resentment was being barely contained.

For several months of individual psychotherapy sessions, this manner never changed, nor did I ever feel comfortable with him. It always felt to me like his suppressed rage was on the verge of erupting, yet it never did. But his family history gave me an understanding of why I was feeling so ill at ease. He was the oldest child and the only son of two Asian immigrants who had grown up poor, but had managed to create a stable, middle class life for themselves through their self-sufficiency and hard work. They were determined that their children would be successful, which meant that they must be focused and disciplined above all else. Indeed, they made sure there was nothing else. The children were forbidden to socialize with the other kids in the neighborhood, because they were all held to be unsuitably low-class, and would only lead them into trouble. Homework was to be done as soon as they came home from school, and each child was expected from a very early age to have a job that earned them money, which was to be turned over to their parents for household expenses. Everyone was required to speak in complete sentences, no slang words were permitted, no opinions could be voiced that contradicted their parents. No wonder Nate was so rigid and resentful; anything normal and natural was forbidden, and nothing but obedience was tolerated.

Despite my growing understanding of the nature of Nate's problems, we were making very little progress in our sessions. I realized that he was unable to reflect on how he felt either in the session or in his life outside my office. All he could do was be obedient. It was pointless to inquire into his emotional life because that was utterly foreign to him, and led only to long logical discourses devoid of any feeling or insight. Partly out of frustration, but also because it offered the possibility of a treatment modality that would target his interpersonal problems, I suggested that we switch to group therapy, with only occasional individual sessions. He agreed to this, of course; I understood that there was virtually no chance that he would contradict me, as that would be unacceptable to him. He was even able to give a perfectly rational explanation of why this would be good for him, given the nature of his issues. All true, but as usual, devoid of emotional content. Still, I felt this might be the only way I could help him get to the underlying conflicts that kept him so angry and out of touch.

Nate's entry into group therapy was not much different at first from his individual sessions. He always showed up on time, participated in a highly intellectualized way, and droned on far too long when he did

4. THE PSYCHOTHERAPY RELATIONSHIP

talk. I could see how socially unaware he was: stiff, awkward, trying always to be polite. I could also see how frustrating he was to other members of the group. They shifted restlessly when he went off on a long tangent as he spoke, and would roll their eyes as he lectured one person after another about how they should solve their personal problems. I realized I would need to highlight the obvious discrepancy between his intent to be helpful and the negative feelings he evoked; I hoped this would help him see what often went wrong in his interpersonal relationships. In group session one day, I said to him "I can see that you're really trying to be helpful. But I can also see from other people's reactions, that they feel that you're putting them down or criticizing them in some way." He erupted. "You're calling me a liar!" He was shaking with rage as he screamed at me. It was a frightening moment for everyone. Nate insisted I had actually said to him that he was lying. When I replied that I never would say such a thing to him, he shouted back at me "I heard you say it! You just called me a liar!" I went around the room, asking each of the group members to say what they had actually heard me say. None of them confirmed his accusation. It was only then that he calmed down.

For the first time in the group, he was reflective and spoke to the point. He remembered an incident from his childhood, when he came home from his paper route, having stopped for once to get himself an ice cream cone. When it came time to hand over his earnings to his father, he was told that there was money missing. Nate denied it, but his father angrily insisted "You're lying to me! I won't tolerate a liar in my house!" He was told he'd get a beating he'd never forget, and his father was as good as his word; the beating left him bruised for weeks. Nate paused, and began to weep, not dramatically, but with obvious emotion that everyone could see. I encouraged the group members to share with him what they were experiencing, hoping that would give Nate a chance to hear that others could actually sympathize with his experience.

Much to everyone's relief, there were no more frightening outbursts in the weeks that followed. But I could see that Nate was withdrawing and becoming more depressed. He was talking less, and seemed much more tentative. I sensed that perhaps he was feeling ashamed after the incident with me, but I decided that given his vulnerability, it might be best to explore this with him individually. After group, I asked if he'd like to begin meeting with me on a more regular basis. He was cautious, but agreed.

After only a few weeks, I was surprised by how different it felt to work with him individually this time around. Unlike our previous individual psychotherapy sessions, Nate was beginning to open up in a more emotional, less intellectualized way. He began to reveal the extent of his fear and hatred of his father, who I now learned beat and humiliated him throughout his childhood. I no longer felt frustrated when we talked. On the contrary, I began to feel a true sympathy for him. I could feel him beginning to trust me in a way he never had in either individual or group sessions. He began to tell me more about his unsuccessful marriage, his difficult relationship with his teenage daughter, an incident long ago when he had been fired from a job after berating a subordinate. There was much less of an edge to him as he talked about these issues. What came through was his deep regret, his terrible shame at being such a failure with people.

In spite of our new-found rapport, Nate's depression was becoming more severe. He was still functioning, but increasingly felt sad, lethargic, and unmotivated to do much. He asked me if he should go on antidepressant medication. I considered it, but said to him "We could do that, and it might help. But I have a feeling that this is something you can handle without it. It isn't that some mysterious depression has dropped on you from nowhere. You're finally dealing with a great deal of pain from your past, and these are very disturbing things to remember, especially remembering how you actually felt. So, in fact these are reasonable reactions on your part. You just need time to work through what's been stirred up. Then you'll feel better because you resolved these old conflicts yourself." He did not seem reassured by my comments, so I added "But in the meantime, I can teach you some skills that may make the process less painful."

What I offered him, in fact, was self-hypnosis. Nothing fancy, but a sort of guided meditation that would allow him to feel more comfortable in his own skin. We went through the guided meditation several times in our individual sessions. Then he began to practice it at home.

It became a daily ritual for him, and he responded to it almost immediately. The intense depression was lifting, which made it easier for him to do the psychological work that would help him heal.

Nate continued in both weekly individual and group therapy for several years. Over time, there were very real changes taking place. In group, he was more patient, thoughtful, and truly insightful than I would have believed possible. More importantly, outside of treatment, his life was improving in a number of substantial ways. His daughter, whom he saw only occasionally and with whom he always felt unhappy and estranged, began opening up to him, calling him up, wanting to spend time with him. He found this unexpected change gratifying but hard to understand. He guessed that she must be maturing. To which I said "Nate, you're the one who's in therapy. She's responding to you." We both laughed; he could feel that was true. He began having more satisfying and comfortable relationships with the people at work, and received a major promotion to a job that emphasized leadership and teamwork. He was in a long-term relationship that no longer sounded rigid and argumentative, as most of his previous relationships had.

THE CORRECTIVE EMOTIONAL EXPERIENCE

Clearly, Nate had benefitted greatly from years of psychotherapy. But what exactly was the critical factor in his healing? I have no doubt that it was his relationship with me. Until the day when he exploded at me in group, there had been virtually no improvement. Therapy with him had been tiresome and tense. Afterwards, over many years, he was able to reflect on his experience, feel deeply, and interact with others in a genuine, interested, and often kind way. It was not some special technique that allowed these changes to occur, but being able to re-experience his rage at his father, have it be accepted by me without retaliation, and then be invited to develop a closer, more intimate relationship. I did not plot all these responses. I thought about, felt, and intuited what he needed, and tried to adapt to his needs as we went along. He could see that I trusted him, had faith in his capacities to grow, and cared for and understood him. I was a stand-in for his father, but a father who treated him with interest and respect.

Psychologists do not have to instruct their patients to project their feelings and perceptions about their parents or other significant figures onto them. This happens naturally, at an unconscious level. This process is known as *transference*. Feelings of love, hatred, envy, competitiveness, erotic desire, dependence, or mistrust are unconsciously transferred by the patient from important people in their past onto the therapist. It doesn't matter whether there is any real resemblance. For example, Nate was much older than I, and of a different ethnicity. Yet it did not impede him from experiencing me as his father- with all the fear, suspicion, and anger that relationship contained. Similarly, in the case of Jimmy, the relationship we were reworking was the one with his grandmother, because she was the most important- and conflictual - person in his formative years.

The transference of old feelings and conflicts onto the therapist is only half the equation, however. If the therapist does not recognize, understand, and react properly to these transferred feelings not only is a crucial opportunity for healing lost, but real damage may be done to the patient. This is yet another reason why all the training components we discussed in a previous chapter - academic preparation, clinical supervision, and the therapist's personal psychotherapy - are so important. It is not easy to be yelled at, dismissed, idolized, or longed for in the process of treating a patient. Yet in deep psychotherapy work, many of these emotions will emerge. The therapist must experience rather than disregard these projected emotions and perceptions, know that they come from the patient, and link them to what has happened to the patient in the past. But even beyond that, he or she must not confuse this transference with the feelings that might occur in a non-therapy interaction. When a patient "falls in love with you" it is not really you that they love. Their love is directed at who you represent to that patient. However gratifying it may be to be seen so positively, or in other cases irritating to be seen so negatively, the well-trained therapist must separate out his or her own reactions from the patient's projections. A therapist who has not thoroughly examined his or her own issues in personal psychotherapy, or has been inadequately

4. THE PSYCHOTHERAPY RELATIONSHIP

supervised is in danger of misinterpreting these intense, often subliminal interactions.

Corrective emotional experiences occur in psychotherapy only when the patient is allowed to feel hidden, unconscious experiences, express them by reenacting them with the therapist, and then have the therapist carefully work with these conflicted feelings in a constructive way. Each part of this process requires careful thought and attention. When a therapist says very little in a session, it often does not mean that he or she has nothing to say. On the contrary, the therapist may be observing not only what the patient is saying and how it is said verbally and non-verbally, but also how what is being expressed makes the therapist feel from moment to moment. Not speaking much gives the patient the psychological space to think, feel, and project what is beneath the surface. Talking or interacting too much may interfere with this unconscious process, keeping the work shallow and superficial.

Similarly, once therapists can see and feel that these unconscious prior relationships are being re-experienced with themselves, they must carefully tease out what parts of that experience can be talked about, how soon, and in what manner. It is not enough to know what is happening; therapists must also carefully weigh how ready the patient may be to talk about it. Sometimes the transferred elements of the old relationship can be discussed as soon as the therapist becomes aware of them. But other times, the therapist may choose to wait until the patient may be more receptive to analyzing this process. The delay may be for weeks or months, even years if the patient's defenses are so strong that bringing these experiences out into the open would only provoke anxiety, scorn, or denial.

How therapists choose to discuss these experiences can matter as much as when they are discussed. Therapists have to find a way to be "in sync" with their patients; the way they communicate with their patients has to connect, rather than distance them. For example, even if a therapist may cleverly detect an amusing slip of the tongue that reveals a transference relationship, it will not be amusing to a chronically depressed, humorless patient. Nor will a creative, artistic patient respond to a logically detailed interpretation from the therapist. Like all intimate relationships, the patient needs to feel that the therapist truly knows them. The emotional tone, style, or choice of words are part of the relationship, and are essential to helping patients receive what may be disturbing or unexpected new understandings of themselves.

Most importantly, whenever therapists communicate with their patients, they must convey respect and compassion. However, it must be genuinely felt, or it will disrupt rather than help the process. Seeking psychotherapy is not something that people generally want to do. It is something they have to do, in order to reduce their suffering. A properly trained, competent therapist understands this, and respects the courage it takes to divulge often embarrassing personal details to another person, especially an authority figure. From the very first contact with the therapist, feeling respect and compassion instead of shame begins a healing relationship. At each step of the process, therapists' genuine concern and admiration allows patients to re-experience themselves as worthwhile, understandable, and competent to work through their problems. This is not technique; it is a relationship that every patient needs. As we have seen, it is not a simple process, requiring a great deal of skill and training on the part of the therapist. But this bond is at the core of psychotherapy, allowing for transformations that would otherwise be impossible.

5. ADDICTION AND RECOVERY

Addiction, at long last, seems to have come out of the closet. It has always been with us: in the late nineteenth and early twentieth centuries there was probably a higher proportion of narcotic addicts than we have today. But so much of it was shrouded in shame and secrecy; addiction was rarely was talked about, much less treated. Indeed, the medical establishment essentially considered alcoholics and other drug addicts as hopeless cases. The problem was left to quasi-religious institutions such as the Salvation Army or to revival meeting miracle cures. Some souls may have been saved, but for the vast majority of addicted people, there was no help at all.

The first widely available help for the general public did not come until 1935. Two "hopeless alcoholics" who had tried for years to stop drinking met in the home of a mutual friend in Akron, Ohio and began to talk with each other about their struggles. They found that by speaking honestly about their problem, admitting their utter failure to control their drinking, and reaching out to each other before they reached for a drink that they could finally stay sober. Out of their experience came a program they called Alcoholics Anonymous.

AA and other self-help programs such as Narcotics Anonymous, Gamblers Anonymous, and Overeaters Anonymous have permanently changed our society. Anyone with an addiction problem now has access to a confidential, free program of support, encouragement, and advice. By attending group meetings regularly and working on a step-by-step program of self-improvement, millions of people every year learn to achieve and maintain a life free from self-destruction.

But self-help programs cannot do everything, nor do they fit everyone. Addiction problems are often highly complex, because every addict is a unique person. Knowing that a person is addicted to a substance or behavior does not tell you everything you need to know about him or her. To treat the addicted person, therapists must not only understand the dynamics of addiction, but how this particular addiction came about in this particular person. Patients who relapse after admission to a rehab program are often characterized as insufficiently motivated. Sometimes that is true. But just as often, they have been inadequately understood and therefore have received only the most superficial treatment. In the cases I am about to present, I hope to impart a sense of how understanding both the addiction and the person matters.

JENNIFER

I first met Jen when she was in her twenties, an attractive, perfectly dressed young African-American woman, who came for help because of a drinking problem. But there was something about her that made an immediate impression. I noticed it as soon as I saw her in the waiting room. "That is the most earnest young woman I've ever seen", I thought. Indeed, she was. It was not just that she felt bad about not being able to stop drinking; she felt bad about everything in her life that was not done perfectly.

Jen grew up in a household where her parents were constantly fighting. When her father drank, these fights often became physically violent. She remembered thinking, even as a young girl, that if she could just do everything right, she could make the fighting stop. Her father complained about the house being a mess, so she would come home from school and start cleaning up right away. She tried hiding bottles, so he wouldn't drink. She got straight As in school, excelled in sports, and never caused a bit of trouble. But of course, the fighting did not stop, no matter how hard she tried. She remembered feeling terribly guilty when her parents divorced, as though she should have done more to keep the family together.

Jen's record of superlative achievements got her admitted to a prestigious college. But despite her obvious intelligence and history of academic success, she always felt inferior to most of the other students. She spent her nights in the library, reading and outlining every book that was assigned, often asking her professors for additional reading materials. This brought her to the attention of one professor in particular, who seemed to take a special interest in her. Hours spent in his office eventually led to dinner invitations, and then to spending time at his apartment off-campus. Jen was so excited that her professor was interested in her, that she didn't allow herself to acknowledge it was becoming an affair. All she knew was that for the first time that she could remember, she felt happy and good about herself. When her professor abruptly ended the relationship, she was crushed. What had she done wrong?

Drinking had never been of much interest to her. She had begun drinking wine with her professor, enjoying the way it added to the excitement of being with him, of being wanted, of being adult. But now, in her despair, she began buying wine and drinking it at night to fall asleep. It was the only way she could get relief from feeling guilty and ashamed over what had happened. Occasionally she would drink too much, and just collapse on her bed. But mostly, she seemed to be in fairly good control, and continued to drink moderately on social occasions.

Upon graduation, Jen took a job in an investment bank, where her earnestness was both appreciated and exploited. Before long, she was working 80-hour weeks routinely, yet fearing that she might be fired at any time. She grew close to another hard-working employee, an older man whose late hours were occasioned by a desire to avoid the unhappiness of his marriage. They became confidants, then lovers, but her guilt over what she was doing as well as the uncertainty of where the relationship could possibly lead brought a return of her insomnia. Again, she turned to alcohol for relief. After months of anguish, and steadily increasing reliance on alcohol, she decided to leave her job and go back to school for an advanced degree in finance.

Life started improving for Jen. With her usual hard work and focus, she plunged into her graduate studies, and was appreciated and encouraged by her teachers. She was able to cut back her drinking, though by now, she was drinking with friends more often. She graduated near the top of her class, and had her pick of positions at several prominent corporations. She fell in love with a very kind and supportive man she met while on an internship, and took a position in a firm that enabled them to be together in the same city. They married soon afterward.

Unfortunately, young associates in corporate firms are often required to work long hours and travel frequently. Some people can handle that stress with equanimity. Jen was not one of those people. She soon became overwhelmed with the quantity of work, the intensity of the negotiations, and the constant disruption of her life. More and more, she came to the end of the day in yet another city, alone and exhausted - and unable to sleep. She was afraid to admit she was overwhelmed, so she told no one of her problem, not even her new husband. Instead, she drank. The longer this went on, the worse her drinking became. She knew she was in trouble, but kept trying to just push though- until one morning she missed a critical client meeting because she was too drunk to wake up. Her employer put her on probation. It was only then that Jen admitted she needed help.

This was the point at which I met Jen. At her first appointment, I said very little, as she spent most of the hour weeping and explaining how hard she was trying to keep her drinking under control. She assured me that nothing like this had ever happened to her before. I had to very delicately suggest to her that while I did not for a moment doubt her sincerity, it was very unlikely she would be able to drink successfully. She said to me "Are you telling me I need to go to AA?" I told her perhaps not, but she certainly showed all the signs of early-stage alcoholism. This was shocking and disturbing to her. Despite the overwhelming evidence of addiction, she tried to convince me that I didn't really understand. Or as she put it, "How can you accuse me of alcoholism? I don't drink every day." To which I said, "Alcoholism is not an accusation; it's a diagnosis. I can only help if I'm honest with you about what we're dealing with."

5. ADDICTION AND RECOVERY

Jen's defensive reaction to the diagnosis of alcoholism reflected a combination of basic lack of understanding, emotional denial, and her particular personality structure, which registered alarm at any sign of disapproval or imperfection. All of these factors had to be addressed in order for her to accept the seriousness of her problem.

Misinformation was the easiest obstacle to address. Most people suffering from addiction require a certain amount of education, since there are so many myths to confront. For example, Jen's statement that she couldn't be an alcoholic because she didn't drink every day is a very common misunderstanding. Alcoholism isn't primarily about how often you drink, but how you drink, why you drink, and what happens to you when you do. In Jen's case, what was diagnostic was that she frequently drank to excess, that the amount and frequency of her drinking was steadily increasing, and that she was becoming more and more dependent upon alcohol to function (for example, to fall asleep). Most of all, the fact that her drinking led to a serious problem at work was so completely out of character for such a conscientious person that it could only happen because she had lost control. These are all classic signs of addiction.

It is one thing for the doctor to be certain of the diagnosis; it is quite another for the patient to accept it. For most other psychological problems, this difference doesn't matter that much, because the diagnosis doesn't drive the treatment. But with addictions, the patient must know and accept the diagnosis, because acceptance of the reality of the disorder must occur before any helpful treatment can occur. The patient may have many unsuccessful attempts to stay away drugs, alcohol, gambling, or other addictive behaviors. Yet until he or she knows and *accepts* that attempts to "do it just a little" are defensive rationalizations, nothing is learned from these failures. Addicts who suffer a setback can learn more about their vulnerabilities, their defenses, and what they need to do in the future to make these slips less frequent. However, this learning occurs only if they accept that the slips have a meaning beyond just bad luck.

Accepting the reality of her alcoholism was a torment for Jen. Despite my efforts to clarify over and over again that her alcoholism had nothing to do with moral weakness, she could not easily accept that she could be an alcoholic and not be a defective person. She tried AA meetings at my suggestion, but hated them because she felt she was different from most of the people she met there. And she certainly wasn't about to go to a meeting that required her to announce her name and say "I'm an alcoholic." She could admit she had "a drinking problem", but that's as far as she would go. As a result, whatever success she had in in not drinking was only temporary; eventually she would end up drunk without intending it to happen, leaving her ashamed at herself for her weakness and lack of discipline.

One Christmas, she and her husband went back home to visit her father and step-mother. Trips home had always been fraught with tension for Jen. She always felt disapproved of, and frequently would end up drinking heavily during some part of the visit. This trip was unexpectedly calm. When she told her father how much happier and easier-going he seemed, he told her he had finally stopped drinking. She asked him why, and he told her "I finally admitted I was an alcoholic, and if I kept going the way I was, I was going to die. So I started going to AA meetings."

At our next session, Jen told me about the surprising trip home, and how proud she was of her father. I asked her if she thought she could do what he had done. She said she wasn't sure she could. "My father's not a perfect person, but he's very strong. I don't think I am. Every time I try to control my drinking I fail. And he goes to AA, which I can't stand. I think he's more disciplined, and stronger. I wish I were more like him. Maybe then I'd be able to stop." To which I said: "Actually, I think you're quite a bit like you're father. You're both very bright, hard-working and successful. But both of you are very stubborn, and reluctant to ask for help. That's why it took him decades to accept that he was alcoholic and do something about it. Maybe you don't have to wait so long." She thanked me for my good opinion of her, but said that I don't see her every day, so I don't know how weak she really is.

At this point in the session, I was beginning to feel the same kind of frustration that I often did with her. No matter what I said, she obstinately refused to entertain a concept of herself as anything other than deficient. It was her own particular kind of conscientiousness taken to the extreme: if something wasn't working, it was her fault because

5. ADDICTION AND RECOVERY

she must not be doing enough, proving that she was weak or lazy. Out of things to say, I took a different tack than usual. "Why don't you ask your husband if he sees the similarity between you and your father? It might help me to hear his perspective."

Much to Jen's surprise, her husband immediately saw the similarities between herself and her father. In fact, what he said to her was almost identical to what I had said, including the points about her stubbornness and reluctance to get help. That got through to her. She couldn't dispute what her husband had said to her; he was the only person in the world she really trusted. This was the opening we needed. She stopped fighting my suggestions and observations, and her denial, born of shame and guilt, was finally loosening. I suggested she tell her husband more about our therapy sessions, and we began thinking of him as a partner in our work. In fact, it became something of an inside joke among us. Though I never actually talked to him, he would often tell her to talk about certain issues with me, and we would laugh at how often his views and mine coincided.

Jen finally stopped drinking, though she never did go back to AA. Her husband and I became her support group, which for her was a better fit to her personality. After several years of work together, she was sober, less anxious, and far happier than she'd ever been. Some years after she'd completed her treatment, I got a note from her announcing the birth of twin daughters. She included an additional note. "My husband is still helping me carry on the work we did. Soon I'll have five years of sobriety."

There's a postscript to this story. After many years of sobriety, Jen had a serious slip, and began drinking secretly. It was very hard for her to admit she was in trouble, and as you would expect, she came in feeling ashamed and weak. But we were able to quickly get her back to doing the things that had helped her before: opening up to her husband, remembering that her drinking was not proof of her inadequacy, learning to recognize stress before she became so overwhelmed that she needed instant relief. She was surprised how soon she was able to recover, but it was clear to me that this was not just luck. Jen now had the tools to function without alcohol; she had clearly internalized all of the earlier therapy, and could accept help if she needed it. Slips often happen even with the most successful treatment. But they are not a sign of failure, just a reminder that recovery is an ongoing process which requires sustained effort.

WARREN

"Do you treat gambling addiction?" was the question posed to me by the caller with the young-sounding voice. I told him I did, and asked if this was about Internet poker. He said it was, which didn't surprise me. In the last ten years, there has been an explosion of gambling websites on the Internet, with a steady stream of mostly young men coming to see me because they were losing huge sums of money and could not stop playing.

What did surprise me was his age. Warren was only 19, a baby-faced teen with a shy, awkward manner. He came straight to the point. "My parents are furious with me. I've been playing online for a while, but they only found out because I ran out of money, and got so desperate I started stealing from them to try and win it all back. It probably would have worked out all right if I had just won. I was hoping I'd recover what I lost and then replace the money in their account before they noticed. But I kept losing." His losses added up to over $20,000.

Warren's pattern of gambling was similar to most of the Internet gamblers I've seen in my practice. They are usually bright young men with a good head for numbers, who start out dabbling and quickly find they can make a lot of money easily. At first it's thrilling. But before too long, they find that no matter how much they win, they can't stop while they're ahead. This was exactly what had happened to Warren. He began playing in high school, and by the time he was 16 had built up a sizable bank account. But it was getting harder and harder to walk away. In recent months, he had lost entire days playing, skipping classes, not eating, and not sleeping until he was out of money. One time, he told me, he started losing purposely, just so he could get to sleep.

5. ADDICTION AND RECOVERY

Warren was not in denial about his problem. He knew he was out of control, knew it was an addiction, understood playing "just a little" was not an option. But he didn't know how he could stop. "It's not like a drug, or something. I can't just stay away from it. The Internet is everywhere, and I need to go online just to live my life. But once I get on, before I know it, I'm on the poker website. It just seems like it happens automatically."

The first focus of our work was pragmatic and tactical. We had to help him develop a daily routine that would minimize his temptation. He agreed to a strict set of rules about when he could go online, and for how long. Discussing his experiences, we were able to break through his conviction that going to the poker website was "automatic." In fact, it was usually preceded by a small lie. "I'll just go online to check my email" or "I need to check out something on Wikipedia," was followed by going directly to the gambling site. I told him that if he did not get honest with himself, he'd never be able to stop. "No one who is really going on to an innocent site has to say to himself 'I'll just' do anything. ' Just' is the first word in your lie to yourself. It's the same with any justification used before acting- 'I need to', 'I only' are phrases that hide the true intention." He protested a little. "But I do need to go to those sites. I'm not always lying about it." Again, I pointed out to him that I understood that, but the clue that he was about to lie to himself came from how he phrased the intention in his mind. Until we were sure he wasn't lying to himself, he would have to restrict his Internet use to a public facility, like a library, where access to gambling sites would be restricted.

I knew, however, that this alone would not stop him from gambling. In order for anyone to break from a destructive addiction, there has to be an understanding of what caused the extreme behavior and what will continue to trigger it. Warren couldn't seem to tell me. But I talked to his parents, and began to have a much clearer idea of the underlying dynamics of Warren's problem. When he was just starting high school, the family was plunged into a terrible crisis. The family lived in a small, tight-knit community in which his father was a prominent businessman, employing hundreds of workers from the town. One day, the police came to the door to tell Warren's father that there was a riot outside his offices. It seems that everyone's paychecks had bounced. He called his bank, only to find that his accounts were completely overdrawn. As it turned out, his partner had embezzled all of the cash in the business just before leaving on vacation. The business was broke, and his reputation ruined. When Warren went to school, he was cursed at and beaten. A police detail was placed outside their house to keep the family from being attacked. The family was forced to move out of town to live with relatives a few miles away.

It took several years for things to return to normal. Warren's parents were obsessed with the need to save their home and business, spending most of their time raising money and repairing relations with vendors, customers, and employees. Family life was completely disrupted, and Warren lost several good friends. Even when they returned to their old house, things were not the same. Warren now spent most of his free time on the computer, where he discovered something that both entertained him and provided a way to help his family financially: online poker. He'd always been something of a math and computer genius, and he figured out a way to play the odds that seemed to be a sure thing. Small bets became bigger, and he was thrilled to see that his system was really working. He told his parents he had started up an online computer troubleshooting business, in order to account for the large amounts of money he now seemed to have. He proudly gave them several thousand dollars to help with their expenses. They remembered feeling proud of him, but terribly ashamed that they needed his help.

All compulsive gamblers will tell you that eventually their luck runs out. After years of playing, Warren started losing. At first he just assumed things would turn around, so he played more and bet higher to recover from his losses. But even when he won, he couldn't stop. Up by $5,000, he would become obsessed with getting to $10,000. This was no longer just a game or a way to make easy money. It was a compulsion that he had lost control of. It wasn't really that his luck had changed; he had changed. He was now an addict. So even when he won, he eventually lost.

When Warren went off to college, his parents still had no idea of his gambling problem. But things soon fell apart. No longer under any

5. ADDICTION AND RECOVERY

adult supervision, he often didn't go to classes, spending days at a time gambling. Sometimes he won enough to pay off his losses, but only until the next big loss. He was getting desperate. On a trip home, he stole his aunt's credit card. By the time that was discovered, he'd found a way to hack into his parent's checking account. The family was outraged, wondering if they should press criminal charges. After all they had been through, they were terrified of once again being plunged into a financial crisis. "How could he have done this to us"?

Oddly enough, it was Warren's aunt and uncle, whose credit card he had stolen who calmed the parents down. They prevailed upon them to see this as a problem that needed treatment, not punishment. That is what led to Warren's initial call to me.

The understanding that I got from talking to Warren's parents was just what I needed to intervene therapeutically. Warren had been unable to see the connection between the family trauma and the development of his addiction. Like most young people, he could only see his problem as his fault; that he was reckless and selfish to have done what he did. But I kept pushing him to remember what had happened earlier, how it felt, what his thoughts had been, why he was so determined to win money for his family. It was not that I thought that once he understood how he felt that he would no longer have a gambling addiction. Of that, there was no question; he was a compulsive gambler who could no longer gamble at all. As such, everything that we had discussed earlier regarding required changes in his behavior and accountability remained true and necessary. Yet I knew it was unlikely he would be able to sustain that kind of discipline if he didn't work through the feelings beneath the self-destructive behavior.

Over time, it became clear to both Warren and me that his addiction had developed insidiously out of the turmoil and pain of his family situation. He felt he had lost everything: his friends, his family, his home. He was terribly depressed and lonely, but there was no one to talk to about it. He didn't feel he could talk to his parents about his problems; they were frantic and distraught themselves. For a while, gambling was the only thing that was positive and exciting in his life, the only time he didn't feel bad. And when he was winning, he felt like he could really do something to make things better for everyone.

He wasn't planning on becoming so obsessed with gambling that he couldn't stop. He just wanted to hold onto that good feeling. He didn't see until much later that he had lost control, and that he would never again be able to feel good in that way.

Talking with me in therapy was a way for Warren to begin feeling better about himself without the adrenaline rush of gambling. He was angry and depressed about everything he had lost, but had never been able to talk about it. He didn't want to blame his parents for his unhappiness, and felt guilty and selfish for complaining. I had to help him see that it was natural for him to be angry about what had happened. It didn't have to be his parents' fault or his fault to explain how he had been feeling. Nor was it wrong to want to feel better. Yet, at the same time he had to understand that as much as gambling had once seemed the answer to his problems, it now had become the problem itself. Feeling better would have to come by talking out his problems with another person who understood and supported him. For now, I was that person.

One of my biggest concerns was that I seemed to be the only person Warren was talking to. With an addicted person, that is always risky. So much of what addicts need is relief from the shame and sense of isolation they feel about their problem. But at best, he could only get this kind of relief once or twice a week when he met with me. For that reason, I suggested that he start going to Gamblers Anonymous meetings. He did find a meeting that he liked, but it only met once weekly, and it took over an hour to get to by public transportation. But as luck would have it, a solution to that obstacle emerged unexpectedly. It turned out that his aunt- the same one whose credit card Warren had stolen-had started calling him regularly to check up on him. Warren hadn't known that this aunt was a recovering prescription drug addict and that she had spent many years going to Narcotics Anonymous. Because of her own experience, she really did understand Warren, his addiction, how bad he felt and why. Warren now found he was able to confide in his aunt in a way that he never could to anyone else in his family. In time, his uncle and aunt were able to help Warren's parents understand their son's situation in a much more compassionate way. So, as I later said half-jokingly to Warren, "you're luck hasn't run out. But it has nothing

5. ADDICTION AND RECOVERY

to do with cards or gambling. Your real luck is in having family who love and understand you."

I worked with Warren for well over a year. During that time, he had no slips, and he continued talking to his aunt several times a week. He had developed the capacity to reflect upon what he was feeling, and had real insight into what had happened to him. Most importantly, he could tell from how he was feeling from moment to moment when he was at risk, and how to reach out to others at those times. But even with this progress, it was increasingly clear to me that he missed his family terribly. With his permission, I talked to his parents about the possibility of his returning home to live with them and go to college nearby. They were reluctant to have him return, for fear that without our regular sessions, he would not have enough support. However, I reassured them that I would remain available for telephone consultations or even regular sessions if necessary. Warren needed to recover the sense of being close to his parents, to recover what had been lost to him. This was an essential part of his healing, and I was certain that it would strengthen his recovery. He now had the tools to maintain his recovery, and I considered his prognosis to be excellent. The occasional emails I have received from Warren and his family since then have confirmed this judgment.

These two cases are fairly representative of the hundreds of patients with addiction problems that I have seen over the years. Although the details of each of their lives are unique, there are some fundamental principles that apply to all of them. I would summarize these principles as having the following characteristics:

1. **All addictions have certain core features.** Whether it is alcohol, other substance abuse, compulsive gambling, or other addictive behaviors, the mechanisms of addiction are remarkably similar. Addictions all tend to start as variations of normal behavior that grow progressively more frequent, extreme, or time-consuming. As the person's involvement in the substance use or compulsive behavior accelerates, the person will start to hide it, revealing a subconscious awareness that something is wrong. But if you ask the person directly about it, the problem will be minimized,

rationalized, or denied. Eventually, a threshold is reached where the sufferer is unable to control what happens when he or she engages in the problem behavior. The person may be able to stay away from it for a period of time, but once started, he or she cannot stop. If found out, apologies will be made, excuses given, promises offered, but they are useless, because the person has lost control of the behavior. This pattern occurs over and over, until finally some external threat-legal action, loss of a job, loss of a relationship- motivates the addicted person to seek help.

2. **Nevertheless, every addicted person is different, and his or her path to recovery will be determined by personal history, personality style, and life circumstances.** Most addicts are ambivalent about treatment. At the conscious level, they don't really want to stop; they just want to get out of the trouble that they are in. But subconsciously, by the time most addicts come in, they know very well that their lives are falling apart because of their addiction. This is, for most people, a painful admission. Motivating the addicted person to want to abstain requires the therapist to understand who this person is, and in what social, psychological, or environmental context the addiction emerged. Only when the patient feels understood in this way can he or she begin to face the problem honestly, without feeling ashamed.

3. **Psychotherapy for addictions requires a more active and direct approach than in more traditional therapy.** From the very first session, the psychotherapist who is treating an addicted person must be prepared to take an active role. At first, most patients will need to be educated about the dynamics of addiction and recovery, and typically there is a good deal of denial that must be confronted. But even more fundamentally, the therapist is involved in helping the patient learn a whole new way of living. Addiction is an essentially passive mode. For people who are caught up in an addiction, overcoming feelings of depression, loneliness, anger, or tension are achieved not by doing something, but by passively receiving a substance or sensation that provides the desired feeling state. Coping

skills atrophy, and the person becomes increasingly dependent on their drug or particular compulsion to get through the day.

Ironically, though we have come to think of addiction as a disease, it actually functions in a very different way than other illnesses. With most diseases, the patient is a passive victim; the patient's actions have very little to do with becoming ill. Accordingly, treatment is a passive process; the doctor treats the patient by writing a prescription or performing a procedure. The only thing the patient is required to do is show up and cooperate with the doctor's instructions. Treatment for addiction is nothing like that. This is because addictions, unlike most other diseases, don't just happen to people; they emerge out of a complicated chain of emotional experiences that cause them to make increasingly maladaptive choices. Paradoxically, though the problem emerges from voluntary choices, addicts do ultimately become passive sufferers, as the addiction takes over their life. When addicted people come in for treatment, to the extent that they consciously acknowledge the problem at all, they experience it as something that has just happened to them. And their expectation is that the doctor will do something to relieve them of their problem. However, the therapist must make it clear that unless the patient is committed to changing his or her behavior, the problem will only get worse. The responsibility rests with the patient, not the doctor.

4. **We treat addiction by showing patients how to depend on people, not on substances or compulsive behaviors.** Human beings are hard-wired to interact with and respond to other people. When an addiction replaces this natural human dependence, a precipitous downward spiral results. As an individual's addiction grows worse, he or she becomes more and more narrowly focused on the addictive behavior, crowding out most other activities, especially with other people. Consequently, addicts often feel desperately isolated, but they have lost the instinct to reach out to another person. Instead, they turn to their addiction for relief of this pain. The result is an endless loop of false hope and misery.

The remedy for this misery is in learning to rely on other people. AA and other self-help programs work precisely for this reason: they target the importance of human relatedness in recovery. That is also the essence of psychotherapy with addictions. As we saw in the case examples of Jen and Warren, attempts at behavior change alone were not enough. What was needed was trusted relationships, both with the therapist and with a family member. In order to recover, addicts must learn that the substance or behavior to which they have become addicted cannot bring them the comfort they long for. But it is not easy to convince an addict of this fact. Drugs and addictive compulsions work instantaneously and require little effort. Relationships take time and persistence. Moreover, these patients are often so demoralized that they no longer believe that another person can understand or accept them. The experience of putting their trust in a therapist who can speak frankly but with sympathy is a bridge back to the world of people. Helping them deepen and broaden those relationships is what ultimately strengthens their recovery.

5. **Recovery is not a cure. Abstinence from the addiction must be consciously and willingly chosen and maintained on a regular basis, or there will be relapses.** The fantasy of most addicted people is that once they stop the addictive behavior, they will be able at some time to resume "normal" drinking, drug use, gambling, or other compulsion. That is virtually impossible. For whatever reason -and we don't know with certainty why this is so- once a behavior becomes addictive, it does not revert to a more moderate form. The addicted person must accept that there is no prospect of moderation; abstinence is the only real option.

It may take some time and several slips for the addicted person to accept this reality. No one wants to believe that they are permanently unable to control some aspect of their behavior. It goes against our normal self-conceptions of autonomy and free will. So these slips are common. What is essential is not that the addicted person never slip, but that these relapses be acknowledged, talked about and analyzed. Only then can they become opportunities for deeper understanding and acceptance of the reality of the addiction.

6. THERAPIST ERRORS AND WHAT THEY MEAN

Like everybody, therapists make mistakes. I am not referring to gross errors or acts of incompetence, which are usually avoidable, but to the small errors of judgment that are inevitable when dealing with the complexities of treating patients. To paraphrase the great jazz musician Artie Shaw, if you are not making mistakes you are not really doing your job. What I mean by this is that to do good work in psychotherapy, the therapist needs to take some risks, to make on-the-spot judgments or to think unconventionally. For competent practitioners, these risks and judgments involve leaps of intuition that often propel the work forward. But sometimes therapists misjudge the situation or encounter blind spots within themselves. In those cases, the therapist's practice of self-reflection is essential, in order to understand what has gone wrong and why.

DOROTHY: AN UNINTENDED REJECTION

Dorothy was a woman in her late fifties who had recently been arrested for her second DWI offense. Her attorney had suggested that she enroll in alcohol counseling; I had seen one of his clients some time ago, and he recommended me as someone who could probably help her.

At our first session, Dorothy admitted to me that she knew she had a problem with alcohol, and that it was getting worse. She knew exactly when the drinking began to be a problem; about eight years earlier, when her husband died of colon cancer. I asked her about her husband's illness, and how it affected her. She curtly replied "How do you think I felt? I felt terrible. How's bringing all that up going to help me?" I tried to explain how often drinking problems are related to emotional disturbances that trigger a loss of control. She interrupted my explanation. "Look, I know I drink too much, and I definitely should not have gotten into my car after drinking. So I need your help to help me stop. That's why I'm here".

Given Dorothy's intense resistance to even thinking about her pain, I felt obliged to only offer her a behavioral program for avoiding drinking. It didn't go very deep, and it barely engaged the emotional foundations that trigger addictive behavior; it might not work. But a person whose defenses are that brittle is sitting on a time bomb that will eventually go off. Any sign of opposition to what she demanded would be experienced by her as an insult. I would need to find a gentle way to help her move in the right direction. This had to be very slow and subtle.

Unfortunately, the program I laid out didn't work at all. She would have a few good days of abstinence, but then she would have some justification in her mind of why it was ok to drink, and she'd get embarrassingly drunk. We went through this sequence perhaps six times before I finally said: "Look, maybe you're not ready yet." I meant it in all sincerity, and hoped she could hear that as a non-judgmental way to acknowledge the failures without characterizing them as shameful or permanent. She was immediately hurt. "I know I messed up. Why do you think I'm coming to you. You're supposed to help me, not criticize me." I apologized for my mistake; she calmed down. We talked amiably for the rest of the session, and talked about some changes she might make in the coming week. We said goodbye, and I said "See you next week", as I often do at the end of a session.

She never came back.

That was my error. Of course she was almost impossibly sensitive to insult. What I said to her was something that I say fairly frequently to other addicted patients. Usually, they find it supportive. But I intuitively knew Dorothy would not. Though I did not intend it to be, she felt it as a criticism. Nevertheless, the fact that it was unintentional does not explain why it happened. Reflecting on my experience, I realized that I had felt frustrated by her right from the beginning, because she denied me the flexibility I needed to provide proper treatment. I accurately read her defensiveness, and modified my approach accordingly. What I ignored was how I felt about it. The irritation, the blow to my professional pride came through, even if mixed in with solicitousness. What she heard was "Go away if you're not serious. You're wasting your time and mine." I misjudged her needs, because I allowed my annoyance to cloud my judgment. It was true that she wasn't ready, but that did not mean she didn't want my help. She just needed me to be even more patient than I was. Perhaps, then, she could talk more about how she felt.

I experienced a little regret about this incident, but not much. It goes to the nature of a therapist's errors. I was attuned to my patient, just not perfectly attuned. I went beneath the surface to interpret her behavior, and what it meant. That much was correct. But she needed me to penetrate to an even deeper level of understanding, one that could accurately recognize and interpret the unconscious effect her defensiveness had on me. Because I did not, she felt misunderstood. Given the nature of her underlying conflicts and defenses, there was no margin for even that little error.

RYAN: A NEAR-MISTAKE, CORRECTED JUST IN TIME

Ryan was a young man in his mid-twenties, who contacted me because of a crisis at work. He had just missed another deadline because of constant procrastination, and knew that if he didn't find a way to break this pattern he would be fired. In talking with him during our initial consultation, I learned that he came from a very dysfunctional family, in which his father beat his mother on numerous occasions. He told me that as a kid, he learned to cope with the violence by crawling into his bed with the covers over his face so he could shut out the sounds of the fighting. Once he was a teenager, he stayed out of the house as much as he could, and then went to college far away from home. He had since held a number of jobs, but had this same procrastination problem at all of them.

I was beginning to get a feel for the underlying nature of Ryan's work problem. Normally for men, the ability to work productively requires that the boy identify with his father as the symbol of competence and confidence. But Ryan could not identify with the cruel and explosive man who terrorized his mother; he wanted to be as different from his father as possible. What he could not know was that in doing so, he might be throwing away the baby with the bath water. Ryan had no work ethic, because that was associated with his father. To succeed in the workplace, he would have to find a different internal role model.

The creation of an alternate sense of oneself who takes pride in accomplishment and daily work is a long, complicated process. I knew I would have to be the transitional father in his life, the man who symbolized the positive value of work, but who was approachable. But we could never quite get around to this deeper work. There was always a work crisis to deal with that could not be ignored. We were talking about techniques for organizing his time, prioritizing, all of the practical strategies that we all need to do our work.

In the meantime, there was an even bigger obstacle. Whenever I saw Ryan, I had difficulty staying awake. At first, I thought of it as a logistical problem; he was my first patient of the day. I tried changing his appointment to a different time of day. It didn't change a thing. I could hardly keep my eyes open. Under those circumstances, the work we were doing was barely competent. I started doubting the value of our sessions, wondering if perhaps I should refer him to a colleague who could do a better job. This certainly wasn't working, and I found it disturbing and uncomfortable to meet with him. How could that possibly be in his best interest?

I was just about to suggest a referral when I realized what my sleepiness meant. *He was crawling under his covers, going to sleep to protect himself from pain.* He didn't know how to do anything else to keep

6. THERAPIST ERRORS AND WHAT THEY MEAN

the painful memories and feelings away. So I was feeling his sleepiness projected into me. That was what he was trying to communicate to me unconsciously: *I can't bear the pain; I have to get away from it.* But he was also communicating the key to understanding why he was unable to work. I had been feeling useless, unable to think, wanting to pass the work off to someone else. That's how he felt. *You can't work when you're half asleep.* He was showing me through his unconscious how it felt to be unable to do your work. That's why I felt so incompetent.

My insight came just in time. I changed course, turning from supposedly practical strategies -that actually were useless- to asking more about the violence at home. At first, he couldn't remember much, but I pressed him to picture himself in the house, in his bed, to tell me in detail what he heard. His usual soft-spoken monotone became more emotional. He remembered the sounds of furniture crashing, of his mother screaming, of his father's loud booming voice yelling obscenities. He talked about feeling pathetic for doing nothing but hiding. I explained to him that it was beyond what a child should have been expected to do. That he was doing what we all do, just trying to survive.

It took several years of weekly therapy for him to work through this entire trauma and develop a healthy outlook towards work. But I never felt sleepy with him again. He was awake and facing his problems, and now I was able to do my work with him. He slowly became much more productive and took increasingly responsible positions.

I often reflect on how close I came to making the serious error of referring Ryan to another therapist. It would have felt like one more failure in his life, and could have permanently prevented him from facing his real problems. What saved the therapy from this failure was the one thing I had been neglecting: asking myself what my sleepiness meant. I had become so focused on being "practical and realistic" that I ignored the data that was hiding in plain sight.

I would add one more comment about this case that goes to the broader meaning of what constitutes a mistake in psychotherapy. For psychotherapists who are not meticulously trained in the discipline of self-observation -and there are unfortunately many of them- none of the data that I eventually understood would have been available. As a result, it is likely that Ryan's treatment with such a therapist would have missed all of the deeper connections that explained his work paralysis. That would have been the biggest error of all.

MALPRACTICE OR MISTAKE: THE CASE OF DOCTOR GREEN

The malpractice suit is every doctor's nightmare. By and large, I believe most therapists are highly motivated to help their patients, and try very hard to provide competent, ethical treatment. But as we have seen, with work that is so complex, errors are bound to occur. A small percentage of these missteps result in litigation against therapists, requiring them to justify what they did and why. A common assumption is that these cases come about because of gross negligence or incompetence. Sometimes that is so, but even more often, they represent a faulty understanding of the therapy process and of what these errors actually mean.

I speak about this as someone who has served as an expert witness in a number of psychotherapist malpractice trials. This experience has given me a rather unique perspective on how and why malpractice suits may occur. One of the surprising things I have learned is that malpractice can be alleged whether or not an error has actually been made, or if a mistake has been made but is relatively minor, or if the error comes from well-intentioned efforts that produced an unanticipated negative outcome. What often matters most is not the nature of the error itself, but the strong emotions that have been stirred up either in the patient or the patient's family. To illustrate this point, I will describe the case of Dr. Green, which was a case in which I testified as an expert. As with the patient case studies, some details have been changed to protect privacy.

Bruce and Lisa, a professional couple in their early 40s, were referred to Dr. Green by Lisa's family physician. Dr. Green remembered them as a very physically attractive couple, who seemed desperately unhappy. Bruce angrily complained of being ignored, of having no sex life, and

6. THERAPIST ERRORS AND WHAT THEY MEAN

that his wife spent too much time at work and at the gym - anywhere but home. For her part, Lisa complained about his loud, angry tirades, his abusive language, and his insensitivity. Dr. Green told them that she would be willing to work with them, but only if they were both committed to trying to change the negative interaction between them. They agreed, and she began seeing them weekly for several months. There were some small improvements, but they were still fighting often. Feeling that they needed more help to reduce their conflict, Dr. Green suggested to each of them that they could benefit from combining the couples sessions with some individual counseling. Bruce dismissively said he didn't see the point; the only thing he was having a problem with was his wife's unacceptable behavior. But Lisa agreed, saying she felt very depressed and asked if Dr. Green would be willing to see her. She said she would, as long as Bruce was comfortable with that; he had no objection.

In the course of her individual sessions, Lisa was more explicit with Dr. Green about just how bad things were at home. Apparently, Bruce frequently screamed at her in front of their two young children, and his outbursts were becoming more accusatory and frightening. That's why she had been withdrawing from him, but that only seemed to make him angrier. Dr. Green asked her if she was afraid he might hit her. She said he had pushed her once, but didn't think he would actually hit her. Dr. Green expressed her concerns about the escalation of Bruce's rage, and that this needed to be discussed in their couples sessions. When Lisa did not bring this up, Dr. Green voiced her concerns. Bruce became enraged, accusing Lisa of lying. Dr. Green tried to calm him down, but was unable to do so. He left the session abruptly, and never came back. Dr. Green called him several times, but he never returned her calls.

Dr. Green continued to see Lisa for a while, but the situation at home was getting worse. One night, Bruce punched a hole in the wall, just barely missing Lisa's head. In a panic, Lisa called Dr. Green, who advised her to leave the house with the children before the violence escalated. She did, and the next day got a restraining order, requiring Bruce to leave the house. When he came back to the house the next day, she called the police, who arrested him for violating the Court order. He never lived there again; Lisa filed for separation, and after a very nasty and contentious legal battle, they were divorced the following year.

That same year, Bruce sued Dr. Green for malpractice. He alleged that she had been biased against him and that it was her advice that led to the breakup of his marriage.

I was asked to evaluate the case as an expert, reviewing Dr. Green's notes, as well as the testimony of Dr. Green, Bruce, and Lisa in sworn depositions. It was abundantly clear to me that no malpractice had occurred. This was the vindictive act of an angry ex-husband, looking for someone to blame. The jury in the case agreed with my opinion, and found in favor of Dr Green.

Nevertheless, in one sense Dr. Green did commit a serious error: she underestimated how pathological Bruce's anger was. When this couple came to see her, this was not just a communication problem or a relationship crisis, the sorts of problems one often sees in couples counseling. This was something altogether different. This marriage was being destroyed by a narcissistic man who reacted to any slight with sadistic aggression. Dr. Green's sympathy towards Lisa- seeing her individually, bringing up the issue of her husband's rage, advising her to leave the house when she was in danger- was interpreted by Bruce as taking Lisa's side against him. At first, his fury was directed at punishing Lisa. But once that fight was over, Dr. Green became his next victim.

The paradox of Dr. Green's error is that it happened because she had done such good work with this couple. We know, with hindsight, that Bruce was an angry, often brutal man who was largely responsible for the destruction of his marriage. But Dr. Green, like most good therapists, was able to see some positive qualities in him, and conveyed her respect for these qualities in such a way that even he felt accepted and understood. How else could one possibly keep a man like Bruce in couples therapy for as long as she did? What disrupted the balance in this case was that once she appreciated how violent the situation had become, she was ethically bound to address it. Detached from Dr. Green's admiration, Bruce was far more angry and defensive. She misjudged his character because it was her own empathy for him that propped him up, making him look healthier than he was. So it was a

6. THERAPIST ERRORS AND WHAT THEY MEAN

mistake. But it was the kind of error that only good therapists would be likely to make. And let us not forget: she probably saved Lisa's life.

ACCEPTABLE VS. UNACCEPTABLE ERRORS

Not all therapist errors are created equal. The missteps that are made because of inadequate training or unethical conduct are always unacceptable, because they are entirely preventable. Practitioners must be honest with themselves about the kinds of patients they are competent to treat and the type of treatments they are providing. Similarly, psychotherapists must always maintain the highest level of ethical conduct; there is no room for rationalizing self-interested behavior. When patients come to see a psychotherapist, they are counting on the therapist's competence and integrity. A therapist who violates that trust is likely to make serious and harmful mistakes. These errors are inexcusable.

Then there are the well-intentioned errors committed by inexperienced therapists, which may result in inadequate treatment. Fortunately, they are often correctable with proper training and supervision. For example, a patient may be receiving fairly competent treatment for depression, including psychotherapy and medication, but continues to struggle. By all accounts, the treatment should be working, but it is not. Perhaps it is because the patient also has a serious drinking problem that the therapist has not considered. Generally speaking, neither psychotherapy nor anti-depressant medication can be effective in a patient who drinks heavily. In time, and with proper guidance, the novice therapist will learn to routinely ask about patients' drug and alcohol use. This kind of error comes from inexperience rather than incompetence. It thus falls in the category of unfortunate but entirely correctable mistakes.

The errors made by properly trained, experienced clinicians tend to be more complex. The most important protection against errors at this level is scrupulous honesty, self-reflection, and consultation with other experienced colleagues when difficulties arise. Still, some mistakes will be made, no matter how conscientious and capable the practitioner. As we have seen, the kinds of errors that experienced psychotherapists make are intrinsically related to the nature of the work they do. In order to deeply engage with another human being and to heal repressed traumas, therapists willingly enter into their patients' psychic world. Relying on their training, skill, and self-knowledge, they navigate within this world, periodically stepping out of it to evaluate and test their hypotheses, and then re-engaging the patient's inner experience. It can never be done flawlessly; mistakes will be made, but these errors are also part of the process. If they are properly acknowledged, the therapist can utilize what he or she has learned to benefit the patient. Both therapist and patient learn from these errors.

7. WHY PSYCHOTHERAPY TAKES TIME

Many years ago when I was young and idealistic, I agreed to participate in a managed care insurance program. I didn't particularly want to be on a panel of discounted fee providers, but I thought of it as a sort of civic duty; a way to reach patients who would not otherwise be able to afford psychotherapy. It turned out to be a thoroughly dispiriting experience. Every patient's complex problems had to be summarized in an absurdly simplified treatment plan, and then sessions would be doled out, five or ten at a time. In order to have more sessions authorized, the progress of the treatment would have to be described in terms of concrete goals and objectives met. None of this remotely matched the patient's experience or needs. To make matters worse, I became unhappy with myself because by these metrics, nothing was happening. No one made any "progress." I felt incompetent, and in a sense I was, because I was doing superficial, bad work.

All of this changed once I realized the impossibility of what I was trying to do. I resigned from the panel, and negotiated reduced fees with these patients so they could afford to stay in treatment for as long as they needed. Instead of some fictitious problem that we were supposed to solve rapidly, we were able to address my patients' actual issues. We took our time, and did real work together. For most of them, this meant years of weekly sessions. But in the end, they received the treatment they needed, and their lives were greatly improved.

I tell this story because I think long-term psychotherapy is frequently vilified as inefficient or unnecessary. Mostly, this viewpoint reflects the insurance companies' deliberate calculations to minimize costs. The insurance companies don't have to pay for long-term psychotherapy if they can, in complete self-interest, declare them to be "unnecessary treatment." In truth, only very limited problems, for example a specific phobia, might benefit sufficiently from brief treatment. The majority of complex problems do not.

Generally, when patients enter psychotherapy, they are struggling with very complicated, life-long patterns of dysfunction. They can describe to the therapist how they feel and what their symptoms are, but they cannot understand why they feel the way they do, or why they can't get better. All of that is buried in their unconscious, which does not operate in a linear, rationally organized fashion. Rather it is indirect, its data written in idiosyncratic codes known only to the patient, but then further obscured and disguised by the patient's own defenses, making the data virtually unintelligible to them. It takes time, patience, and skill in order for the psychotherapist to decode and then address these complex problems. Short-term, problem-solving techniques don't address them at all.

In the following case study, I will try to demonstrate how and why long periods of time are often necessary for the transformative process of psychotherapy to work.

CARLOS

It wasn't easy to begin working with Carlos in therapy. Not that he was uncooperative. He always came precisely on time, never missed a session, and didn't question that he needed professional help. But unlike with most of my other patients, I was having a very hard time getting an understanding of how he felt. Nearly everything he said was stated factually, as though he was talking about someone else. There were plenty of words, but no emotion. Even his face was singularly unexpressive.

7. WHY PSYCHOTHERAPY TAKES TIME

To hear him tell it, Carlos had been through some tough times, but everything eventually worked out. His parents immigrated to this country when his mother was pregnant with him. The family had very little money. His mother died when he was three, shortly after the birth of his younger sister. His father was overwhelmed with taking care of the kids, so he and his sister went to live with his aunt and uncle and their children in a neighboring state. They were hard-working and religious, "strict but fair" as he often put it, and he learned about responsibility and self-discipline from them. At first, his father visited fairly often, but as the years went by, it was just a few times a year, then hardly at all when he took a job half-way across the country. But by that time, it didn't matter that much to him; he figured his aunt and uncle were like real parents to him and his sister. What difference did it make?

It was very odd listening to this type of unemotional, unreflective account.

"How did your mother die?"

"She was very depressed after giving birth to my sister. I think the doctors call it postpartum depression. She ended up taking her life."

"My God, how terrible. Do remember how you found out, or how you felt when that happened?"

"To tell the truth, Doctor, it was such a long time ago, I don't really remember. Anyway, I don't think I knew it was suicide until I was an adult."

"And then your father left you?"

"No, no. He didn't leave us. He just couldn't cope, so he took us to live with my aunt and uncle. It wouldn't have worked, because he wasn't strong enough to deal with raising two kids on his own. It was a much better situation for all of us."

For the longest time, that's how our sessions would go. I would learn the facts of his life in some detail. How he excelled in school, got both an academic and an athletic scholarship to the state university, played college football, married his college girlfriend. That he earned a degree in engineering, took a job with the Federal Government, and eventually left to establish his own successful engineering firm. That he'd been married for twenty years, and had children of his own. I learned a lot about his product line, the problem of attracting and retaining good employees, managing the growth of his firm, bidding on contracts.. He could tell me a lot about his children, what a good mother his wife was, where they went on vacations. But I knew very little about how he felt about all of this. It didn't help to ask: he had nothing to say. When he and I were in session together, it seemed that I was the only one with any feelings, and mostly I felt empty and depressed.

So why was he in therapy? Because at the age of 42, he had a heart attack. He didn't have many of the risk factors for heart disease: he didn't smoke, drank very moderately, exercised regularly, wasn't overweight. His physician concluded that he needed to reduce the stress in his life, and referred him to me. Carlos was reluctant to call, but his wife begged him to follow through. It made sense to him that reducing stress would be a good thing, and his wife had been so scared that he felt he needed to do something. So he agreed to come.

Given that he had only come to psychotherapy because other people thought he should, one would think that he would be a very reluctant patient. But strangely, he was not. He always kept his appointments, and when either he or I had to be away during our usual appointment time, he always tried to reschedule. That fact alone made me suspect he must be feeling *some* comfort or support from therapy, even though he could neither show it nor tell me so. There were some other incidental signs of improvement. He slept through the night more often, rather than awakening early because he had too much on his mind. His wife had told him that he didn't seem as preoccupied. Still, after three years of weekly sessions, that was about all the progress I could see.

During our fourth year together, some cracks in the armor emerged. These were subtle shifts, but revealing nonetheless. One day, I announced that I would be away for a week later that month. He was uncharacteristically silent for what felt like a long time. Then he asked how he could reach me if he needed to. He had never asked that before. I told him that, as I always do, there would be a colleague covering for me while I was away. He asked who it was, and took down

7. WHY PSYCHOTHERAPY TAKES TIME

his name and phone number. He asked a few more questions about this colleague. I answered his questions, but also asked him why he was so interested to know this information. Again, silence. Then he lectured me on how unprofessional it was for me to "leave your patients in the hands of a stranger." He also travelled on occasion, he told me, but at no time was he out of phone contact with his family or staff.

This interaction signaled to me that something very significant was happening. Carlos was beginning to feel some strong emotions, though he could not yet acknowledge or even know that this was happening. But I understood: he was angry at me for abandoning him. Of course, that's not what he said, nor would he have explained his feelings that way. But unconsciously, that was his coded message to me. If we break down the elements of his communication, it will be easier to see how I was able to decode this hidden message:

My announcement that I would be going away in a few weeks was nothing new. He had been in therapy with me for four years, and I had been on vacations several times each year, each time giving notice in the same manner. But this time, he became silent when I made the announcement. The silence, especially for such a long time, suggested that he was having an emotional reaction to what I had said.

This was followed by his asking how he could contact me. For someone so guarded and inflexibly self-reliant, this was very unusual. He would never consciously admit that he needed anything from anybody. It was really contrary to his entire personality structure to allow himself to depend on me. In effect, he was involuntarily blurting out this hidden need.

His questions about the credentials of the colleague who was covering for me were asked in a rote manner, and he seemed completely uninterested in my answers. It was quite clear to me that there was some other reason for these questions. I answered his questions out of courtesy and respect. But since I knew they were not the real questions he was asking, I inquired as to why he was asking. Silence again, which reinforced my sense that strong emotions were being suppressed. Then a scolding tone, as he implied I was being unprofessional, by which he meant not behaving in his hyper-responsible way.

But why was this happening and what did it mean? After years of talking to me every week, Carlos' long-dormant longings to be taken care of were beginning to emerge. He had not allowed himself to feel these emotions since childhood. And with good reason. He had been abandoned twice: once by his mother's suicide, a second time by his father's disappearance from his life. But of course, *that was a long time ago, Doctor. Anyway, it all worked out for the best...* That was the story he forced himself to believe, so he would never have to feel the pain of these wrenching losses. But as with most defense mechanisms, his desperate need to choke off painful realities came at a high cost. He didn't just shut off the pain, he shut off all his emotions. That's why I always felt so empty and drained during our sessions; I was experiencing what it was like to be emptied out of all feeling.

Accusing me of irresponsibility and neglect had tremendous emotional resonance for Carlos. Not that there was any truth in the accusation, at least as applied to me. But as a stand-in for his parents it was spot-on. Of course, his parents obviously had terrible problems of their own. But their actions caused great suffering for their children. Carlos' moral outrage was therefore entirely justified. As I became the proxy for his parents, he could finally begin to feel the outrage of their irresponsibility.

However, his emotional awakening was just in the beginning stages. This incident between us occupied perhaps two minutes, and did not immediately change anything. I listened patiently to his complaint, expressed regret that I hadn't considered he might want to contact me directly, and gave him my personal phone number. Through it all, there was just a flicker of emotion, and no hint of recognition that his disapproval of my behavior had anything to do with his parents. Nor did I suggest that connection; I knew it would fall on deaf ears. It was far too soon to expose him to feelings he'd spent his whole life avoiding. So the moment passed, while I waited for his emotional development to reach the point where such painful reappraisals could be tolerated.

The following year, there were other emotional shifts. However, they were not in my office but at home with his wife, Denise. For the first time, I began to hear complaints about her. Carlos felt she was becoming moody and argumentative, in a way he had never seen

7. WHY PSYCHOTHERAPY TAKES TIME

before. They had a fight in front of the children; he knew that was terribly wrong, but he could not get her to stop arguing with him. She was criticizing him constantly. He wondered if she was going through early menopause, because she seemed so different, and so emotional. He had no idea why she seemed so unhappy, especially with him. I listened to all of this for many months, trying to get him to think about whether there might be some truth in her complaints about him, or whether he might be provoking her in some unintended way. He was sure he had done nothing wrong; he was the same as ever.

Finally, I asked him whether he thought a consultation for the two of them might help. He thought that was a good idea. Who would do that, he wanted to know. I remembered his earlier complaint about *leaving your patients in the hands of strangers,* and offered to provide the consultation myself, if he was comfortable with that. He was agreeable.

Several weeks later, we had our first couples session. As often happens, Denise had a very different story to tell. It was not she who was becoming more emotional and irrational; it was Carlos. He was coming home from work irritable, complaining about his employees, then about the untidiness of the house, and about his teenage son spending too much time on video games. But worst of all for her was his micromanaging of everything. It was true, she admitted; she was arguing with him much more, and she regretted raising her voice in front of the kids. But she was sick of his complaints, and of how controlling he was.

The discrepancy between their accounts did not trouble me. On the contrary, what Denise said made perfect sense. Of course it wasn't she who had changed; it was Carlos. He was more irritable and emotional because he was no longer suppressing everything he felt. So for the first time in their marriage, he was difficult to live with. Just as I had seen in our individual sessions, Carlos was feeling angry and impatient with the supposed irresponsibility of those he cared about: his wife, his son, me. But as in our individual therapy sessions, he was unaware of these changes in himself. Without this self-awareness, he could only see Denise's responses, not his changed behavior, and so he blamed her for suddenly becoming so difficult. It was totally distorted, but not random. Something very important was shifting in him: his explanations may have been wrong, but he knew that something didn't feel right. In that sense he was correct; something indeed was very wrong. His tidy, unemotional story about his past was falling apart, and his irritability reflected the pain of that faint awareness.

It wouldn't have helped at all to explain this to Carlos. He was still just feeling angry; he had no conscious awareness of what his anger meant. So I didn't bother. However, having him in the same room with his wife, confronting a problem that reflected his deepest emotional issue was an opportunity not to be missed. I began by acknowledging the obvious: they had a serious conflict, but with very different views about what was really happening. Would they like to work the problem out together with me? As I suspected, even with their very different perspectives, they were both eager to have me intervene. Each of them was desperate to be heard, to have their position validated in front of their partner. We began to meet weekly, adding a different layer of potential understanding to Carlos's weekly individual psychotherapy sessions.

Having Carlos and Denise agree to an extended period of counseling was an undeniably valuable opportunity, but only the first step. What did I intend to do to help them? I was not really interested in problem-solving, or making their life more peaceful. That would be a common-sense approach, but one that would provide almost nothing of real or lasting value. In a sense, I was far more ambitious for them, and for Carlos. I saw this as an opportunity to reveal to him, at both the level of internal feelings and in interaction with his wife, how his traumatic early experiences were interfering with his ability to enjoy his life. And for the couple, I saw it as a chance to move them beyond a stale compromise that kept them stuck at a level of interaction that allowed for little growth or development for either of them. To be honest, they weren't asking for this. But I took a calculated risk, based on what was by now a deep understanding of the situation and of Carlos's character. He was nothing if not courageous. Look at what he had done to survive and ultimately to succeed in creating security for himself and his family. I felt that he would understand and appreciate my faith in him, and my willingness to be bold on his behalf.

7. WHY PSYCHOTHERAPY TAKES TIME

I spent many years with them in weekly couples therapy. Though we dealt with a multitude of conflicts, my focus was quite singular. I listened very carefully to each of them; their fears, frustrations, and aspirations. Then I translated what I understood to their partner, using my knowledge of their personalities and conflict areas to provide the most sympathetic explanation of their needs to each other.

Simultaneously, in our individual psychotherapy sessions we often took extra time to digest what was happening in couples therapy. I also listened for opportunities to link what he was learning emotionally to a reconsideration of his past. All with a light touch, out of consideration of the pain it would stir up. Occasionally, there were incidents within the therapy sessions themselves that helped make those linkages explicit. For example, one month Carlos wrote a check to me that bounced. When I mentioned it to him, he became upset and defensive. "That's not possible. There must be some mistake. I always make sure there's plenty of money in my account." To which I replied, "I honestly don't know how it happened, and I'm not concerned with placing blame. I just wanted to point it out to you, as a straightforward financial matter. You know, it's part of how anyone runs their business, attending to these things. I'm just telling you so you can take care of it." The rest of the session went haltingly. I knew he was still upset.

Sure enough, in our next couples session, things had blown up. Carlos had gone home and pulled out all of the previous month's credit card statements. Then he grilled Denise about each expenditure, complaining about how her spending was excessive. This had the expected effect of provoking a terrible argument, as she resented his patronizing accusations. In the session, she told me that she had done her own research, and found that he'd forgotten to deposit his paycheck at the usual time. That couldn't be true, he said. "I always make that deposit right on time." That was too much for Denise. "Look at the fucking bank statement! You didn't make the deposit! Can't you ever be wrong?!!" She was about to storm out of the office, but I persuaded her to sit down. I asked to see the bank statement, and had her show me how she could tell a deposit was missing. Then I said to Carlos, "She's completely right. There are only three weeks of deposits, not four. You made a mistake. It's not the end of the world, but it's your mistake, not hers. You really can't blame her for causing the check to bounce. For that matter, you don't really need to blame yourself. It's something we all do."

What I said next was unexpected, but something I'd thought to myself many times over the years. "Carlos, you really must learn the difference between a simple human mistake and an action that is morally irresponsible. Forgetting to make a deposit or accidentally banging up the car is not a big deal. But abandoning your young children, leaving them to fend for themselves, is really unforgivable." My heart was pounding. I knew I had finally voiced the unspeakable, after eight years of patient waiting for the right moment. "What are you saying?" Carlos said, in a tone more defensive than curious. I turned to his wife and said "Denise, I think you know exactly what I mean." Without any hesitation, she said "You're talking about his parents, and how terrible it was what they did to Carlos. You just can't ever talk to him about that." Carlos said nothing, so I continued to talk to Denise. "You're absolutely right. But you have to understand what that does to a child. It's so overwhelmingly painful, so awful that you can't even let yourself think it, let alone feel it or say it. So it ends up coming out sideways. You end up blaming the people you love for things they didn't do, or getting angry about other people's irresponsibility all the time. It's wrong, but you really have to be big enough, loving enough to see how much pain he's in. He doesn't know what he's doing."

Denise moved closer to Carlos on the couch. She put her arms around him, and just held him. No one said a word for a few long minutes. Then we ended the session.

Over the next few months, both the individual and couples sessions became noticeably different. If I were to describe the difference, I would say it felt much less like hard work and more like thoughtful, intimate conversation. All of us had been constrained by the pressure to work around the trauma of Carlos' childhood. Now it could be referenced, and whatever problems came up between Carlos and Denise could be examined in the light of how that trauma was spilling over into the present. It was same in his individual sessions. We didn't have to talk around the issue, and I didn't have to be so careful and indirect. None of which meant that the work went quickly. The issues of abandonment and irresponsibility were everywhere: at work, at home, even in the way he thought about politics and the economy. But at least now we could get to the heart of things.

One of the biggest changes was that both Denise and I could begin to make sense of his workaholic behavior. His hyper-responsibility was now more understandable as a defense against being anything like his parents. In time, he began to see that what drove him to work so hard all the time was not "a proper work ethic" but fear of being irresponsible. Delegation was impossible, if that meant he was abandoning his responsibilities. But if he could learn to make that distinction, he could finally begin to let go responsibly. At one point, I actually suggested that he let Denise handle the family finances. Both of them resisted the idea. I pushed back, saying to Denise "You can't really say you support him doing less if you continue to depend on him to do so many things that you know you can do yourself." I knew from the years we'd spent together that Denise had come from a family in which her father was frequently unemployed, and her family constantly struggled to make ends meet. No wonder she'd been so attracted to Carlos: he would never let that happen to his family. So they had an unconscious pact that provided them both with a sense of security they lacked as children. Except that the agreement was killing Carlos, perhaps literally. It was time for both of them to move to a more adult kind of relationship, one based on interdependence and partnership, rather than simply assuaging their childhood fears.

After roughly five years, we began tapering off the couples sessions. Their relationship was so much happier and more open that there wasn't much need to meet. Carlos continued for several years afterwards in individual therapy, consolidating his insights, and continuing to make changes in his lifestyle. He now had a much more balanced life, spending more time with family and friends and less time at the office. More importantly, he looked and felt like a real person. He could laugh about things that were happening around him, and he was far less judgmental and stiff. When at one point he actually missed an appointment, something that would have been unthinkable years earlier, he himself commented on that as a sign that he was feeling ready to stop coming. He hadn't quite known how to tell me; we both laughed, knowing that what he was telling me proved how much he had changed. He now understood precisely how his subconscious worked; how being afraid to tell me ended up being expressed indirectly by his "forgetting". It was an awareness that once would have been unimaginable. At our last session, this huge, onetime college football player, this man who once could not have recognized an emotion, gave me a big hug and a touching, heartfelt goodbye.

Short-term therapy is an appealing idea. Like much of what we most admire in our society, it fits with a preference for precision engineering and technology. Why not design psychological treatments that have the same scientific rigor as high-tech medical treatments? Instead of years of talking, shouldn't it be possible to quickly pinpoint the problem, explain it to the patient, provide the patient with a set of tools to continue working on the problem, then send the patient on his or her way? It seems direct, efficient, and pragmatic. But most of the time, it is a fantasy, because such protocols bear no resemblance whatsoever to how the human mind works.

I understood Carlos's problems quite well within the first few sessions. At the behavioral level, he was a workaholic whose levels of stress were becoming dangerous to his health. This in fact is what his physician recognized, and wisely referred him for psychotherapy. However, this was only the top layer of his problems. The diagnostic issue that mattered most was *why was he so stuck in this destructive behavior?* His rigidity, lack of emotional expressiveness, and especially the oddly blithe way he described his childhood all revealed the meaning of his compulsiveness. Carlos was a man so deeply traumatized by parental abandonment that he was unable to function in any other way. He had to embody extreme responsibility, to distance himself from any connection to his shockingly irresponsible parents. It was a desperate strategy, constructed by a young child who had no other way to cope. It worked: he survived. But at a crippling cost.

That, in human terms, was a precise and comprehensive psychological diagnosis. It addressed the observable behaviors, the underlying dynamics, and the etiology of the disorder. The treatment plan I devised was no less precise. My objective was to help him become less compulsive about work and his responsibilities so that he could begin to have some enjoyment in his life. In order to do that, he needed to understand why he could not let go of his responsibilities. That, in turn, required him to be able to re-examine his past, to acknowledge his terrible pain and losses, and to redevelop his capacity to feel and acknowledge his emotions. Without all of that, he would remain trapped in his hyper-responsible compulsions.

What might make this treatment plan seem inefficient or imprecise is that the psychotherapy took so many years to complete. This in fact has nothing to do with inefficiency. The amount of time required to adequately treat a patient in psychotherapy is mostly determined by the patient's personality structure and defenses. It is not up to the therapist to determine how long the process should take. The therapist follows the patient, observing the changes in his or her capacity to address increasingly difficult issues. If the patient is not ready, pushing forward will not help, and may often hurt the patient. In this respect, psychotherapy is much like surgery. We do not ask a surgeon to do a complicated twelve-hour procedure in four hours. We understand that the difficulty of the procedure determines the length of the surgery. To demand otherwise of the surgeon would not increase efficiency; it would be butchery.

Ultimately, concerns about how long psychotherapy takes often come down to cost. Long-term therapy is undeniably expensive. But so is a university education, open-heart surgery, or the cost of raising children. We all make choices to pay these expenses if we feel they have real value. For Carlos and Denise, insurance covered only a fraction of their costs for over a dozen years. They did not question the value of these expenses. Neither did the many friends and family members they have referred to me over the years. They accepted the long, slow, often expensive process of psychotherapy or couples therapy only because it dramatically improved their lives. I do wish that more people could afford long-term therapy. But that is a public policy issue, hinging primarily on whether our society decides that providing high-quality, long-term therapy is sufficiently beneficial to warrant public subsidies. For my part, all I can do is maintain the highest standards of care, so that every patient I see gets the care he or she deserves. I cannot pretend that providing short- term, cheap treatment is an adequate substitute.

8. HOW PSYCHOTHERAPY HEALS

*I*magine this common situation: a three year-old boy is lying in bed when he is awakened by the sound of a thunderclap. Frightened, he runs from his bed to his parents' room, saying "Mommy, Mommy, I'm scared!" The mother rouses herself from sleep, takes the little boy in her arms, and says to him in a soothing voice "It's all right sweetheart. It's just a thunder storm. The loud noise is called thunder and the flashing lights are lightning. That's what happens sometimes before it starts to rain." Sure enough, soon the little boy hears the sound of rain falling. He begins to relax, then falls asleep in his mother's arms. She walks him back to his room, tucks him into his bed, and then she returns to her bed. In the morning, he awakes, perhaps not even remembering what happened during the night.

This small incident is so ordinary we do not realize what a miracle of evolution it represents. Unlike most other animals, human beings are born utterly dependent upon their parents, and remain so for a very long period of time. There is a good evolutionary reason for this. An animal that is born able to survive on its own within a few short weeks will necessarily have to rely almost entirely on instincts, not learning. Its biology is its destiny. Human children are quite different, not reaching maturity and self-sufficiency until the late teens or longer. This prolonged dependency confers enormous benefits. The longer the child's brain is exposed to learning from experienced elders, the more intelligent, nuanced, and adaptive he or she will be as an adult. This is true both for cognitive and emotional skills. We learn to regulate our emotional states, manage fear, communicate our needs, and trust others largely through years of interacting with our mothers and fathers.

The little boy in our story has just experienced a major step in his development. Frightened by an unfamiliar, loud noise, he ran to his mother. She accurately read his distress, explained what the frightening sound was, and used both words and physical contact to soothe him. She kindly and generously took the time to allow him to regain his composure and relax into sleep. Knowledge, language, confidence, trust, emotional resilience, and relaxation were all taught, seamlessly and without fanfare.

Now let us imagine the same situation, but with a very different parental response. The mother wakes up, and says in an annoyed tone "It's the middle of the night! What are you doing up?" She hears the boy's description of the frightening sound, and says "That's just thunder. Go back to sleep." She turns over and hears him crying. Angrily, she gets up, and walks him back to his room. "Now go to bed", she says, closes the door and walks out of the room.

Or this response: the mother wakes up, takes him into her bed, and goes back to sleep. No words, no soothing. Later that night, her husband turns over, wakes her up and initiates sex. Perhaps he doesn't notice that a child is in the bed with them, or perhaps he doesn't care. The mother doesn't say anything to her husband, but perhaps assumes that the sleeping child will not notice.

The latter two scenarios represent the dark side of children's long dependence on the care and guidance of parents. The very quality that makes us such an intelligent and adaptive species makes us vulnerable to all sorts of psychological disturbances. Without the attentive care and comfort provided by good parenting, children grow up bewildered, anxious, angry, impatient, despairing, and unable to calm themselves or control their impulses. These deficits don't develop because of just one negative incident of course. But the incidents I've described are often representative of a whole style of parenting that characterizes the way that the parents relate to their children. Given a lifetime of such damaging interactions, the child in the second scenario, for example, is likely to grow up to be an angry, anxious, or drug-dependent adult. The child in the third case, a pedophile or psychopath.

Every patient has a developmental history that shapes who they have become. If our patients came to us recounting incidents like the ones I've just described, it would be relatively easy to know what has gone wrong. But that almost never happens. These incidents are often long forgotten or repressed. Furthermore, even if they were accessible to consciousness, most people would not recognize them as significant events. Instead, the properly trained psychotherapist must watch and listen carefully, to deduce what in the patient's experience has caused his or her dysfunctions. As I have described elsewhere, this is very specific kind of attending to the patient. The therapist must observe the patient's behavior, words, emotional tone, themes, and defensive reactions. Then the therapist must observe how he or she feels in that patient's presence, notice what thoughts and emotional reactions emerge, and sort through both logical and intuitive understandings of the patient to develop preliminary hypotheses. Over a period of weeks or months, these hypotheses are refined, so that the psychotherapist comes to have a quite complex understanding of the patient's unique experience and suffering.

THE HEALING PROCESS

Only when the therapist has thoroughly assessed the nature of the patient's problems can a healing process be initiated. But what is it about the therapy process that heals, and how and why does it work? Or, as some patients will ask me, how is it possible that simply talking about your problems changes your life for the better? In previous chapters, I have illustrated many of the components of the healing process: transference, the reenactment and corrective reinterpretation of childhood feelings within the therapy session, the careful deconstruction of defense mechanisms, the therapist's recognition and response to the patient's unconscious communications, among many others. But even these are just pieces of the process. How can we explain, in general, how healing occurs?

If we return to our initial example, we may begin to understand. The good mother (or, as it has been helpfully described as *the good-enough mother*, lest we think this must be done perfectly) profoundly affects her child through the quality of her interactions. Recognizing distress, tuning in to the child's state of mind and needs, finding appropriate language to explain and soothe, and inducing a state of comfort and security all come relatively naturally to the good-enough mother or father. And just as importantly, the child is naturally receptive to all of these parental inputs. This is one of nature's miracles. We are all built to respond to the ministrations of the helpful authority. In one's family, this is called parenting. In the doctor or psychologist's office, it is called healing.

We should not mistake the healing that takes place in the doctor or psychologist's office as just acting like a good parent. It contains some similar components, but there are fundamental differences. Most importantly, unlike parents, the therapist is a total stranger at first. He or she must actively and deliberately engage with the patient in a way which evokes the receptiveness to healing; it is not reflexive or automatic. For this to happen, the therapist must rely on every type of knowledge he or she has acquired through training: academic preparation, supervision, clinical experience, and personal psychotherapy. These skills must then be married to the therapist's talent at connecting deeply with others. Over time, the competent therapist will have evoked the patient's own self-healing and soothing processes. He or she can now talk directly both to the patient's conscious and subconscious minds.

One way that I know that a patient has entered that receptive state is by carefully noting the patient's non-verbal behavior. It is difficult to put into words, but there is a look that sometimes comes across a patient's face that signals both that they are feeling something deeply and that their defenses have relaxed. It may only last a few moments, but if those moments are recognized the patient may have access to thoughts and memories that had been forgotten or covered up. A similar state may occasionally occur between parents and children who are in sync, but it occurs more or less accidentally. With a therapist, it is induced by all of the work the therapist has done to create an optimal

8. HOW PSYCHOTHERAPY HEALS

healing relationship. The therapist is not inducing this state directly; it arises spontaneously usually after a long period of working together in therapy. But when it occurs, the attuned therapist can recognize it as an opportunity to take the work to a deeper level.

I remember a moment in my own therapy when this healing state emerged. Years after my first experience in therapy, I decided to work with a different therapist, a psychologist whom I had heard speak at a professional meeting. I was by now remarried, and though I knew I had chosen the right partner, it was clear to me that my understanding of intimate relationships was impaired by my early family experiences. I intuitively knew that I needed the help of a female therapist to work on these issues. My new therapist was an exceedingly able clinician, but just as importantly, a deeply genuine person. Our work was going very well, and I had the chance to reexamine my relationship with my parents and my sister. Several years into the therapy, I met her at the door to her office, where she said to me, as she often did "It's nice to see you." Unexpectedly, I teared up when I heard her say these words. She noticed, and immediately and kindly asked what this reaction meant. It was a profoundly moving experience. I could feel her concern and attentiveness, something that was so different from being with my mother. For the next several sessions, we were able to talk very directly and emotionally about what this meant for me, and how the absence of these qualities in my mother had affected my ability to be fully open to love and affection. For the first time in my life, I understood what this meant. This realization was induced by my relationship with my therapist; but the opportunity would have been missed had she not been so attuned to me.

It would be far simpler if once this deep state is evoked, the therapy could stay at this level. But each piece of this profound work must be absorbed and assimilated by the patient, on his or her own schedule. The patient's receptiveness at any given moment is subject to change, sometimes moving forward, sometimes pausing or even regressing. The psychotherapist carefully tracks these fluctuations. The patient talks, the therapist listens in a distinct way: following the patient's conscious and unconscious messages, allowing for thoughts, feelings, memories, associations to take place within the therapist's own mind that deepen understanding of the patient. Comments and interpretations of what the patient is experiencing are communicated throughout the process, but at many different levels. Like the attuned parent speaking to his or her child at different developmental stages, the therapist's explanations and modes of communication evolve as the patient evolves.

Timing and patience are essential. The competent therapist is at least as interested in whether the timing of the communication is right as in the content of the comment. A brilliant interpretation is useless if the patient is not prepared to hear it. So the therapist watches and waits. A properly timed and communicated interpretation allows patients to access their own healing and self-soothing mechanisms, much as medical treatments activate the patient's own immune system. In this way, the therapist's interventions become far more powerful; not as the agent of healing, but as the catalyst for self-healing.

I am tempted to say at this point: *and that's it. That's what healing in psychotherapy is about.* But that would be a little disingenuous. It's a little like the story of the famous Rabbi Hillel from the time of Jesus. He was asked by a Roman official to stand on one leg and explain the Torah to him. *"Do not do unto others what is hateful to you,* he said. *"The rest is interpretation."* Yes, all the psychotherapist has to do is attend carefully so that he or she can find opportunities to speak to the patient's subconscious directly, and thereby activate the patient's self-healing system. All that takes is everything the therapist knows and is.